Praise for *I Always Did Like Horses & Women*:

A fascinating story...I enjoyed the book and admired the research.
   —Lorraine Bonney, historian and co-author of the ten
   Bonney guides for Wyoming, Kelly, Wyoming

Cal's story is marvelous...a fascinating look at a man, revealing a complexity of character not appreciated in the legends about him. The author really brings Cal and old-time Jackson to life...Should be on every Western aficionado's bookshelf.
   —Jeanne Anderson, owner of Dark Horse Books,
   editor of *Spindrift: Stories of Teton Basin*, commissioner
   of the Idaho Commission on the Arts, Driggs, Idaho

The author has done an admirable job of fleshing out Cal's story and establishing him in his own right as a truly colorful and historic figure...Cal moves between different cultures with remarkable ease and aplomb, but never loses his authentic Western character...a welcome addition to the histories of the Valley.
   —Joe Arnold, artist and mountain climber,
   grandson of Felicia Gizycka, great-grandson
   of Eleanor "Cissy" Patterson, Laramie, Wyoming

The author has diligently researched Cal Carrington's life... what a great job! Wish I could have met Cal; he was a rare and authentic person...a truly unique character of the Western past.
   —Doris Platts, Jackson Hole historian,
   author of eight books on Jackson Hole
   and Western history, Wilson, Wyoming

Enoch Layser (signature)

I Always Did Like Horses & Women

Enoch Cal Carrington's Life Story

Orphaned Immigrant, Old Time Buckaroo
Professed Horse Thief
Teton Valley and Jackson Hole Homesteader
Forest Ranger and Dude Wrangler
Guide and Rancher
Socialite, Gadabout, Raconteur
and
Jackson Hole Legend

Earle F. Layser

This book is dedicated to Pattie,
my loving wife and unequaled companion
on life's myriad trails —
together we roamed the West
and shared a grand passion for
the Tetons and Yellowstone.

The Chapters of Enoch Cal Carrington's Life Story

Acknowledgments

This history was four years in the making. During that time I became indebted to many for the use of published works, shared personal knowledge, freely given insights, helpful criticisms, technical support, patience, encouragement and friendship—to all those who lent a helping hand, my sincerest thanks.

The discovery of two unpublished transcripts from earlier recorded interviews with Cal Carrington—one conducted at the University of Wyoming by former U.S. Senator and Wyoming Governor Clifford Hansen of Jackson, Wyoming, in 1957; the second arranged by Attorney Harold Forbush of Rexburg, Idaho, and administered by Teton County Court Recorder Dwight Stone in Driggs, Idaho, in 1958—contributed greatly to this work. Those individuals deserve credit for their insightfulness in conducting interviews fifty years ago in order to preserve Cal's unique history and the times he represented.

A number of Cal's friends, acquaintances and others captivated by his colorful character wrote about parts of his life. These included Struthers Burt, Nathaniel Burt, Harold Forbush, Wendell Gillette, Felicia Gizycka, Eleanor "Cissy" Patterson and Cissy's three biographers: Paul Healy, Alice Albright Hoge and Ralph Martin. These published works are a rich source of tales about Carrington and his life, which if they had not been recorded, most likely would have been lost to time.

I gratefully acknowledge the information shared by those I interviewed and talked with who had personally known or crossed paths with Cal Carrington: Farrell Buxton, Harold Forbush, Oren and Eva Furniss, Bertha Gillette, Gene Gressley, Clifford Hansen, Charlie Peterson, Monty Piquet, Johnny Ryan, Russell Stone, Margaret "Muggs" Shultz and Grant Thompson. Many of these folks were getting along in years, but were all eager to talk about Cal. They provided insights and previously unknown or unrecorded material. Oren Furniss could still saddle and sit a horse at age eighty-nine in 2007. No doubt Cliff Hansen and Charlie Peterson could do the same when they were that young, too.

My sincere appreciation and thanks to those who contributed their valuable time to review my various working drafts and offer their comments, criticisms and edits: Flat Creek Ranch owner Joe Albright, Dark Horse Books owner Jeanne Anderson, Cissy Patterson's great grandson Joe Arnold, historian and author Lorraine Bonney, *Teton Magazine* publisher and editor Eugene Downer, historian Doris Platts, former director of the Jackson Hole Historical Society and Museum Robert Rudd, Fall Line Design owner Karen Russell and three anonymous reviewers of early drafts arranged by Jackson Hole Historical Society and Museum Director Lokey Lytjen.

My discussions with Washington, D.C.-based biographer Amanda Smith occurred late in my work, but proved immensely helpful. She kindly shared knowledge and important primary source materials from her biography in progress on Cissy Patterson, which left me scrambling to incorporate information up until the last moment.

Staff, curators and historians at a number of museums and historical societies assisted me with archival research and in providing photographs: The American Heritage Center at Laramie, Idaho State Museum at Boise, Jackson Hole Historical Society and Museum at Jackson, Teton Valley Historical Center at Driggs, Lee Whittlesey at Yellowstone National Park and the National Archives. I also gratefully acknowledge information received from state and local courthouse records and archivists at Teton County, Idaho, and Wyoming; San Diego, California; and Cheyenne, Wyoming.

Because rumors of horse rustling play such a big part in the folklore of Cal's early years in Jackson Hole, as well as his propensity to declare himself a "horse thief," I want to make special mention of authors and historians who researched and recorded early day horse-thievery accounts in and about the Tetons, upon whom I relied: Mark Anderson, Robert Betts, Frank Calkins, Orrin and Lorraine Bonney, Benjamin Driggs, Doris Platts, Nollie Mumey and Charles Wilson.

I owe a great deal of thanks to Karen Russell of Fall Line Design for her ideas, patience and work in setting up the book's layout, design and cover jacket and for her technical expertise in making this publication a reality.

Last, but far from least, for my wife, Pattie—who has also authored and published articles about Flat Creek Ranch and associated Cal and Cissy legends—I'm grateful and fortunate to have her unfailing support and her willingness to listen and engage in critical discussions. Her support, empathy and professional suggestions greatly aided me in surmounting the many challenges and hurdles that arose while producing this work.

Finally, this history is based upon the interpretations, judgments and research of the author, as well as his attempted artful and selective weaving together of varied source materials. Any resulting omissions, inaccuracies, mistakes or failures in its telling are solely the responsibility of the author.

Earle F. Layser
Alta, Wyoming

Preface

My first glimpse of the compelling Yellowstone–Teton landscape was as a young boy in 1947, while vacationing with my parents. We were what the locals called "tin-can tourists," camping out of an old panel station wagon in the sagebrush. One morning in Jackson Hole a horseback rider approached, and my father, who had cowboyed in Johnson County, Wyoming, in the early 1900s, apologized profusely for trespassing on what he assumed was ranch property. The rider spat indifferently and said, "Doesn't matter; it all belongs to Rockefeller anyway."

I didn't return to Jackson Hole again until my career took me there in 1976. Back then, thirty years ago, Jackson still seemed authentically Western, peopled with genuine and unpretentious folks – the classless society that characters in this book applaud. Where else would a U.S. Senator walk up to a stranger in the airport and start a conversation as Cliff Hansen once did with me. The Hole has since undergone unprecedented change. While this history provides a look at earlier times – people's lives, events and society – it also affords perspective on the inevitable "progress" we as a society have known and undergone.

Originally, I intended to only write a short article about Cal Carrington, a legendary early day Jackson Hole figure. Straightaway, I was foiled by outrageous tales, conflicting myths and whopping information gaps. The more I researched and learned, the more unrealistic the idea of doing the subject justice in a short story became. For instance, previously, gaps in the knowledge of Cal's whereabouts sufficed to substantiate that he was indeed engaged in outlaw activities – if you didn't know his whereabouts, he was off stealing horses. I hesitated to simply repeat old conjecture and handed-down yarns without some verification.

Next, I found "facts" about Cal invariably exist in multiple variants. An eager editor wanting to show their worth at fact-checking could wallow in the contradictions. Some simple examples: Cal's birthplace has been variously given as England, Norway or Sweden; his real name was reported as unknown, changed at immigration's Port of Entry, changed because he was hiding something or derived from a cowboy he admired; popular hearsay claims he belonged to a gang of horse thieves, all of whom were captured except for Cal – yet no records of outlaws being captured for the place and time exist.

Many such issues were resolved by my research, but parts of Enoch Cal Carrington's life will always remain a mystery – lost in the murk of time, confounded by those who realized history could be used to manipulate how the past would be remembered or muddled by canards thrown in just for entertainment.

It's true, too, that if powerhouse Eleanor "Cissy" Patterson had not come into Cal's life, it's unlikely that much, if any, of his history would have been recorded. He would have been just another cowpoke passing through. Cal himself admitted to Earl and Sadie Harris, in Driggs before his passing, that without Cissy and her daughter Felicia, he would have had nothing; Cissy and Felicia were his family.

Nevertheless, while Jackson Hole fondly celebrates Cal's romance with Cissy to this day, it turns out that she and Felicia were not the only important women in his life. He also carried on long-term relationships with Mary 'Mamie' Ake of Mountain Home, Idaho, and Goldie Chisman of San Diego.

Cal's relationship with Mamie remains a puzzle. Was she the young cowboy's sweetheart for whom he had an unrequited romantic notion, or did she in fact bear his child out of wedlock, as some evidence in the Lake Forest Patterson Family Papers may suggest? On his deathbed Cal referred to Mamie as an "old pal," and bequeathed half of his substantial estate to her.

And what about Goldie? He kept in touch with her for over thirty years. Felicia knew about these women and even details of Cal's relationship with them, yet she was discreetly and purposefully silent, disclosing little or nothing about them in her writings.

I've let Cal tell parts of the story in his own words (and spelling), such as his descriptions of working on open range cattle drives in Chapter 2. I chose to describe the entire ten-year saga of Cal's Desert Entry at Bates in Chapter 5, rather than interweaving it throughout the other parts of his life during that same time period. I felt this would more clearly demonstrate what Cal – and others of the time – went through in order to prove up on a Desert Entry. It wasn't "free land."

Some of the likely origins of outlaw tales frequently associated with Cal are revealed and traced in Chapters 6, 7, 9 and elsewhere. From what I discovered about Cal's early years homesteading in Bates, Idaho, and his working for the infant Yellowstone National Park and U.S. Forest Service (see Chapters 5, 8-10) he appears to have lived a much different life than the traditional outlaw lore and legends previously led one to believe.

Many details of Cal's history still remain open to supposition. For example, when Cal, at age 16, allegedly beat up the Mormon elder and ran away from his Utah foster home, it seems unlikely that he lit out on foot. He had to have acquired a horse somehow to have traveled to the Arizona cow camp. Did he vault bareback onto one of the elder's horses, grab a fist full of mane and gallop off – thereby, also, stealing his first horse? Unfortunately, we only know that somehow he made his way to the cow camp, where, as he later claimed, "he learned to ride."

Intriguing parts of Cal's life still remain to be filled in by additional research, a novelist, screenwriter or the reader's own inventions, perhaps. However, Cal's life story need not be embellished to make it fascinating; it's a rousing tale of a life lived to the utmost during rapidly changing times in the American West. This is a book for people who love the history of the Old West and that of the Yellowstone-Teton region, and who will derive inspiration and joy from a true story of a life passionately lived – a spirited tale of an illiterate and orphaned saddle tramp who overcame all odds.

I Always Did Like Horses & Women

Enoch Cal Carrington's Life Story

Left: Enoch Cal Carrington as a young cowboy, c 1908.
Courtesy of JHHSM, 1958.2224.001.

Prologue

Come gather 'round wranglers
and we'll tell us some lies
of cowboys and horses
and bright starry skies...[1]

Hidden deep within a steep-walled cirque, Jackson Hole's Flat Creek Guest Ranch lays nestled beside a glittering tarn dominated by Sheep Mountain. Within the rim-rock confinements, eagles soar and shaggy moose loll. It is a breathtaking place, but not really a suitable spot for a farm or ranch, but then its original claimants had no real intention of making it into one. It's always been a secluded mountain hideaway, a place of legend, where outlaws hid their stolen horses.

Access to the ranch hasn't improved much, if any, from when horses and wagons plied the narrow canyon road. One must buck the last four rocky miles in high-clearance four-wheel drive. That's the authentic way present-day owners, Joe Albright[2] and Marcia Kunstel, prefer to keep it. However, once there, the setting and accommodations are incomparable—original owner Cissy Patterson called it "the most perfect place."

Joe and Marcia adopted a dinnertime tradition; they recount the myths surrounding the ranch's origin. As the sun dips below the rim rock, the extraordinary tales unfold and the lodge's historic photographs and artifacts come to life. The star characters captivate the guests: Eleanor "Cissy" Medill Patterson, a red-headed countess, heiress and socialite; and Enoch "Cal" Carrington, an old time buckaroo and self-professed horse thief.

Biographers have scrambled to chronicle Cissy's life. As the publisher and editor of the *Washington Times-Herald*, she was once considered the most powerful woman in the United States. Cal is generally treated as a chapter in her flamboyant life. However, Cal's life story—he liked to declare his earliest childhood recollections were as an orphan in an Arizona cow camp[3]—is shrouded by early day Jackson Hole myth, and is itself a compelling saga possessing the grand sweep of a sprawling Western epic.

The American West spawned some fascinating and astonishing tales and Cal's life story ranks among those. When he was a young child, his zealous Swedish parents gave him up to serve a religious movement. As an immigrant orphan child in America, he was swept along with the nation's westward manifest destiny. He grew up and lived under rugged frontier conditions among reputed outlaws, but was destined to capture the fancy of a wealthy benefactress who introduced him into high society. Cissy's and Cal's involvement is considered one of the most romantic and renowned cowboy-dude affairs that Jackson Hole, if not the West, has ever known. Cal toured abroad, hunted big game in Africa, and outlived an era. In his later years, he chose to return to his frontier roots and frugally live what appeared to his neighbors to be a simple rural existence; in reality, he maintained two separate lives.

Cal was a young man at a time when the West was still raw frontier. He witnessed incredible change. His life was one of polar contrasts: from farm hand to bronc rider, cattle drover and government horse packer to ranch owner, homesteader to southern California seaside property owner, subsistence hunter to big game hunting guide to African safari, cash poor farmer to socialite, and tight-lipped rogue to sociable raconteur. The romance of his story is inseparable from that of the early day mythos and history of Teton Valley, Idaho, and Jackson Hole, Wyoming.

Cal's family possessed no land or wealth, and judging from his alleged mistreatment and impoverished childhood, no modern day psychologist would have held out much hope for him. From humble beginnings, however, he proved a man was not bound by what he was born, but that in the egalitarian society of frontier America one could attain whatever he had in himself to be. Cal was an orphaned and illiterate cowboy who overcame the odds to realize the American dream of unlimited possibilities. Of course, his meeting a wealthy patron along the way helped some, too. And so the extraordinary life story of Enoch Cal Carrington unfolds—a tale that goes beyond imagination.

1

Orphan Beginnings

Cal Carrington, whose real name was Enock Kavington Julin, was born to Gustof and Julia Augusta Julin on February 10, 1873, in Orebro, Sweden. He is thought to have been the first of five children born into this shoemaker family.[1]

Latter-day Saint missionaries seeking souls to join an American pilgrimage found the Julins to be eagerly receptive. In a zealous show of faith, Enock, at age six, was given up by his Swedish shoemaker family to the care of Mormon missionaries proselytizing under the direction of Albert Carrington, an Apostle of the Council of Twelve and presiding authority over European missions.[2]

When the time came for his mother to hand Enock over to the Missionaries, he cried and clung to her out of fright. Julia, who was quick tempered and torn by her own feelings, knocked him down. He was quickly swept up by the promoters and carried away weeping. According to doctrine, Enock's soul at that moment entered into and became sealed to the Saints' religious movement, the belief being that the souls of children under eight are not fully formed and they are still innocent.

From Orebro, the missionaries and new believers returned overland to the coast and then traveled by ship to Liverpool, where converts from the European Mission converged before sailing on to New York.[3] Enock's passage was undoubtedly financed through the Permanent Emigration Fund Company, supported by the Church's ranching operations on Antelope Island at the Great Salt Lake. It was operated expressly to assist and encourage immigration of converts. The Apostle Albert Carrington also presided over the Fund Company.

Enock's family was to follow later when conditions and finances permitted. But as it turned out he would never see them again until his siblings reconnected with him nearly seventy-five years later. By then, he was in his eighties, and the parents were long since deceased.[4] Enock's father, Gustaf, succumbed to chronic Bright's disease in 1917. His mother, Julia, died in 1919, reportedly of intestinal parasites. Both are buried in the Salt Lake City cemetery. A sister, also named Julia, was listed as an inmate of the Utah State mental institution at Provo in the 1930 census.[5]

Albert Carrington, Enock's namesake, had a distinguished career with the Church of Jesus Christ of Latter-day Saints. But he was also a polygamist with many wives. As a consequence, the Mormon Church excommunicated him for "lascivious conduct and adultery" in 1885.

After the Atlantic crossing to New York by steam vessel,[6] the emigrating Saints, with young Enock in tow, boarded the

Union Pacific railway for Utah, the "promised land" where the "golden spike" had been driven ten years earlier at Promontory. A more romantic version might have him instead traveling by sailing ship to America. Indeed, one of Cal's fanciful tales was that he had been taken onto a "sailing ship."[7] The use of covered wagon and carts on the overland trail by emigrant pioneers mostly ended after the transcontinental railroad was completed.[8] The railroad shortened what had been a six month trip to less than six days.

The fact Enock was given up to strangers by his real family in Sweden and then taken to a distant and foreign country where he had little or no understanding of the language—English became a second language for him—was understandably an extremely frightening and traumatic emotional experience for him as a child. He harbored a lifelong bitterness toward his family for it. His virulence was reflected in refusal to even proclaim his true country of origin, when, years later, he sought U.S. citizenship. Instead he renounced fidelity to the King of England.[9]

It was a Latter-day Saint practice in those days for an adopted child to be "sealed" to the foster parents in the Temple at Salt Lake City, which according to Mormon belief was the equivalent of an "earthly" or legal adoption.

In any case, Cal always facetiously maintained he ended up as an orphaned child in an Arizona cow camp, "where the men would dry their hands on my long curly hair after the evening wash-up."[10] More to fact, he was first taken in by—or you could say "farmed out" to—a Utah family at Smithfield, north of Logan. There is also some reason to believe that his foster family may have later been among settlers dispersed by Brigham Young to the Boise Valley at Mountain Home, Idaho, when Enock was eight years old.[11]

In popular psychology's parlance, Enock had "issues." He was no doubt a stubbornly angry and resentful adolescent. His foster parents allegedly raised him under harsh impoverished frontier conditions with little or no formal schooling. He resentfully claimed, "My education was on the back doorstep."[12]

His childhood, we might conclude, consisted of the day-to-day, dawn-to-dusk drudgery involved in frontier subsistence farming and homesteading, amply salted with religious fervor and righteousness: fetch wood, carry water, milk the cows, feed the livestock, clean the stables, irrigate the fields, put up hay, pray and attend the Ward's—a Latter-day Saint administrative unit presided over by an appointed bishop—church gatherings.

In his later years, he reminisced: "I rode my first bronc when I was fifteen." In reality, it was an unglamorous event. A plow horse he was riding to the field began bucking. Enock clutched and hung onto the flapping harnesses, bull-headedly sticking with the big draft horse until he quit. "But by God I stayed with him," he proudly exclaimed. "I was the tickeledest kid ever!" From that incident, an identity as a horse breaker and bronc rider took seed.[13]

In his own words, he "hated" the stern Mormon elder who was the head of his foster family. Time passed and Enock grew to be a stalwart youth, as his physical stature in adulthood later testified. "At age sixteen," he confided years later, "I beat the hell out of the S.O.B. [elder] and run away."[14]

He never forgave his real family—or Mormons in general—although in his later years he was generally on good terms with some of his Latter-day Saint neighbors in Teton Valley. However, instead of being diminished by his painful childhood, he developed a strong instinct for survival and a hard as nails self-reliance; others called it "a tamped down anger which sometimes surfaced as a hatred for the human race."[15]

Years later, in an interview, when asked where he was born, he retorted: "No. I don't know where I was born. You got something else there? That [subject] is out."[16] In his final years it became obvious he did know, but he remained resolutely reticent on the subject of his childhood all his life, until near the very end.

2

Open Range Cattle Drover

As a runaway, Enock drifted south, an orphan saddle tramp riding grub line. Around 1890, he ended up in Arizona: "I was down there bumming around when I was a kid, y'see. That's where I started out, learned to ride."[1]

Characteristic of him, and no doubt reflecting the soured feelings he harbored for his family, he chose his own name, California, after a cowboy he admired. At some point, he shortened California to Cal, adding the last name Carrington. He was fond of playing with his name, and even tried the sobriquet Calvin, a takeoff on his given middle name, Kavington, perhaps. It's uncertain why, ironically, he chose to take the name of the Mormon Apostle Carrington, who was no relation. The Apostle may have befriended or impressed him in some way. He kept Enock for a name, but somewhere along the way, the spelling became changed to Enoch; perhaps by the immigration port authority when it was recorded on his entry. He even tried "Eunuch" at one point, because he said he liked the way it sounded, but a friend carefully called his attention to its meaning.[2]

Generally, he used the name Enoch, rather than Cal, in his early business dealings, or C.E. Carrington and E.C. Carrington, as documents show. But most of all, he became identified as Cal Carrington, or as his friends called him, Cal.

Beginning at age sixteen, Cal independently and solitarily roamed the western frontier from Old Mexico to Alberta, working as a cattle drover, herding livestock from the Southwest up into Canada. He became a top cowhand and bronc rider.[3] Late in his life, when asked about his early day bronc busting, Cal replied, "They was rough treatment, but I had to make my living some way."[4]

On one cattle drive pushing longhorn cattle from the Southwest up through Colorado to Helena, Montana, "Slater and Twodot" were said to have been the cattle owners. "They took about two years...making less than twelve miles a day.[5] What [laggards] the first herd left [behind], the trail herd picked up," Cal remembered.

"If there was no noise, the cattle was nervous... jackrabbit or anything and off they'd go. I believe that stock likes music...Oh God yes, we sung to 'em. After you've been on herd three to four weeks you ain't hoarse [from singing] anymore. Oh, my God, no," Cal responded to a question on fences, "there was no fences [back then], we didn't even have corrals to rope in...It was wide open country...with buffalo bones still lying around.

"When they got to Helena, they [the owners] had a row among themselves over strays...they said thar was eight hundred head of strays [missing cattle]," Cal recalled, "and Twodot shot Slater and killed him [when he found out]. I didn't see it, but I was thar...a little bit north and west of Helena, on a creek."[6]

Cal allowed that it was easy to lose cattle on those drives with "three to seven thousand trailing along...cows and calves drop out...one man's got a bunch of cows over here and that animal gets in that bunch...and if the man rides looking for something of his, it's fifty-fifty whether he'll see his own animal." He added, "Course, I didn't know nothin' about rustling cattle at that time [as a kid], but since then I've learned a few things.[7]

"The boys would take a notion to go in to town along the trail once in a while and have a little celebration, sorta 'hurrah the town'," Cal called to mind. "If they destroyed anything or shot a light or two, they always paid for it. The bartenders or saloon managers hardly ever objected."

Asked if some of the boys celebrated quite a bit? Cal replied, "Yeah, I've heard tell quite a bit." Characteristically, in his telling, it was always the other guy, not Cal.

Asked, "When a cattle drive ended, did the men ride through the town real fast discharging their guns," Cal responded defensively, "I was never a desperado."[8]

Along the way, cattle sometimes ended up being driven past and right through homesteads, which irritated the farmers, to say the least. Cal commented, "Well, I never seen a quarrel, but I heard some of them cussin'...About as big a stir as affected me was one day passing along a farmer's place with our cattle, there was some tame green head ducks.

"The cook says to me, 'Bet you can't hit one of them.'

"I had an old cap and ball six-shooter loaded with shot. I killed one of them and the farmer came up and about eat me up. So the boys had to take him apart—little stunts like that about happened every day."[9]

Enduring the less romantic side of a cowboy's life was a part of it also: short pay; ten to twelve hours a day in the saddle; chuckwagon fare—beef, beans and bread; extreme weather; sagebrush for a bed; tents and drafty cabins for shelter; dangerous and unpredictable horses; and saddle sores on both horses and riders. Cal said, "Half the time I just slept out on the ground...and if it rained, I'd just let it wash me and the dirty camp bedding out."[10]

Still, he became proficient at skills that served him his entire life—riding, handling livestock, all aspects of ranching, and most of all getting along with some pretty rough characters.

By the late 1800s, the railroads had penetrated inaccessible parts of the West and it became unnecessary to drive cattle long distances to market. Cal had been engaged in open-range cattle drives as that era of the American cowboy was coming to a close.

Similar to his childhood years, Cal generally did not discuss his early buckaroo and saddle tramp days much, or if he did, he didn't get into details—the University of Wyoming interview above was one exception. Invariably, this has been interpreted that he was hiding something. Perhaps he was, however it seems unlikely. We'll never know for certain.

One thing for sure though, he never frequented or even passed through Jackson Hole in those earliest years.

Taming a bronc.
Courtesy of American Heritage Center, University of Wyoming.

3

Horseman and Cowboy

Who was this man, Cal Carrington? It might be said that he lived multiple lives over the course of his lifetime. Perception of him, often contrasting, changed with the places, people and times. No one description alone is satisfactory, but if an image must be chosen, it might best be taken from his early years as a Western horseman and cowboy. It's an image that most certainly would have pleased Cal, too.

As an adult, people were inclined to photograph him— vacationing dudes, ranch owners, socialites, friends, and historians—all did. There is an uncommon amount of photographic portraiture of him over his adult life chronicling his appearance from that of a grinning, mischievous-looking young cowboy to a strapping, handsome man with neckerchief and leather cuffs, to a middle-aged man in a formal suit with silk socks and tea cups, sitting next to a groomed poodle and, toward the end, a cantankerous and colorful character, appearing somewhat disheveled, who hung out in the Wort Hotel in Jackson—an oldtimer who had outlived more than one era. These are some of the known recorded images of Cal Carrington over the course of his life which are included here.

When Cal first rode into Teton Valley, he was a young cowboy, yet his demeanor and mannerisms already commanded people's attention and comment. He stood out from the average man both in appearance and competency. But this, along with his rugged and handsome looks when combined with a tight-lipped countenance and solitary nature, often inspired and elicited fanciful rumors and small-town gossip about him.

As a grown man, Carrington was over six feet tall, nearly two-hundred pounds, with taffy-colored hair, clear blue eyes, a narrow-waist, great chest and large hands—a ruggedly handsome and powerful man. Jackson wrangler Rex Ross once pointed out that, "While Cal didn't look like a real tough guy, he was; he was afraid of no one."[1]

In his heyday in Jackson, when he dressed up, he wore silver-studded leather cuffs and a black and yellow neckerchief tossed airily over one shoulder. Along with a tall cowboy hat and spurred high-heeled boots, he presented an imposing figure. Later in life, in formal attire, he was still a dashing figure summoning respect.

The Burt family, who authored numerous novels in Jackson Hole, patterned their Western characters after him, including Kathrine Burt's cowboy figures in her book *Branding Iron*. In Struthers Burt's *Diary of a Dude Wrangler*, his character "Nate" was based on early impressions of Cal:

Nate was from Arizona...he wore big spurs, high-heeled boots covered with fancy stitching, chaps of leather or angora wool, flannel shirt, neck handkerchief and sombrero...[he] had been a cowpuncher all his life and had to the fullest extent that curious baffling...pride...[which can make] a man with whom you have camped and slept and talked leave you suddenly without a word of explanation... sharp as moonlight and as cold as a knife.[2]

Cal epitomized the glamorous image of the competent Western horseman. Nathaniel Burt considered Cal to be an archetype:

...lank, sardonic, profane and dictatorial, with an aura of glamour and expertise...[he] treated horses with a mixture of affection, callousness, care, amusement, irritation... with a low steady drone of curses... [and] grave deliberation in all movements derived from dealing with spooky animals; [there was a] quiet quick sureness in each act of horse catching, saddling, mounting—precision, economy, grace, effectiveness.[3]

Struthers Burt penned a narrative further reinforcing the image of Cal's superb horsemanship:

Riding across the country with Cal at dusk, when he was in a hurry to get back to camp or the ranch, was an experience to be remembered. Shale rock, fallen timber, gullies, grass slopes so precipitous that a horse sat down on his tail were nothing to him;

Cal Carrington with leather cuffs and neckerchief, c 1916.
Courtesy of Joe Arnold and family.

adding, "There wasn't a horse he couldn't gentle nor ride...[he was] the prototype of the old time cowboy."[4]

People also read into Cal's taciturn nature a reckless or dangerous side, which added to his mystique. Cissy Patterson's initial impression was that he "reminded her of a wolf—lone, savage and quick on his feet." In her 1926 novel *Glass Houses*, Cissy modeled her taciturn and darkly brooding character "Ben" after Carrington. In her story, she has him jealously and very coolly murder a long-standing rival. Cissy describes the rivalry as "two dogs quarreling over a bone for years;" the "bone" being a woman called "Mary"—a composite representation of herself.

One sometimes gets the feeling that Cal was a man who'd give you his last dime, but the next time he'd break your neck instead, and you'd never know why he had done either one. It was said, "Anyone who wanted to make friends with Cal had to make the initial overture, and then he might, or might not, reciprocate."[5]

On the other hand, perhaps because of his being orphaned and without family, evidence points to Cal being very loyal to those he considered his friends or neighbors. He maintained strong, lifelong friendship with some. For those people, he would go the extra mile to do considerate or helpful things.

Cal's words, when he chose, could be "cuttingly laconic or sardonic."[6] Some say he taught himself to read and write,[7] which is partly true, no doubt. However, from his friend Felicia Gizycka, we also learn of a person in his life named Mary Frances Ake, a well-educated and much younger woman at Mountain Home, Idaho. Felicia claimed Mary Ake nursed Cal when he had Rocky Mountain spotted fever and taught him some of his limited reading and writing skills.

Cal's signature on documents is a practiced bold calligraphy, and he readily carried on correspondence in letters—"splashing some ink," as he referred to it. He also owned and used what he called a "word machine"—a

Cal Carrington in Western garb resting on a log
while his horse waits nearby, c 1920s.
Courtesy of JHHSM, 2004.0102.602.

typewriter. Cal's spelling, however, was "creative;" akin to spelling in the original journals of Lewis and Clark. Still, Felicia characterized him as "barely literate."[8]

Enoch Carrington

Enoch Carrington's bold calligraphic signature, June 1901.

Cal was a man of polar contrasts and contradictions. He successfully integrated into high society in midlife, yet at the same time, in Teton Valley, he was considered by some as a "kinda rough guy who'd seen rough times, certainly not a Sunday School boy."[9] Nathanial Burt referred to him as a "wild man, who added spice to the Bar BC setup, especially for the dude girls."[10] Yet, conversely, author Bertha Gillette described Cal as "jolly...never known to be without a broad smile."[11]

Cal, like many Westerners in those times, was skeptical of government red tape and procedures. He made a lifelong practice of avoiding or mocking it whenever possible. He didn't leave a trail, intentionally or otherwise, if he could avoid it. For whatever reasons one wants to imagine, he appeared skittish about drawing attention to his name or doings. It went against his grain.

It's probably no accident that his name doesn't appear in any early census records for either Idaho or Wyoming. But his "it's none of their business" attitude could not avoid paper trails associated with, for example, his Desert Entry claim, Forest Service employment, the WWI draft register, his 1906 National Forest Homestead Act paperwork and other real estate transactions. The frequently manipulative manner in which he went about satisfying paper requirements demonstrated a discomfort with, or scorn for, such things.

Reminiscent of nineteenth-century adventurers, Cal had an incredible wanderlust. Some might say he was always searching. His lifetime of roaming boggles the mind—from Sweden to America; throughout the Intermountain West to Yellowstone; from the West Coast, Southwest, Midwest, and East Coast to Canada, Europe, Africa and even the goldfields of Nome, Alaska. All before commercial air.

When Carrington first came into the Teton country he was a young buckaroo, vigorous and energetic, good at what he did and raring to prove it and that's how he's best remembered: a roguish cowboy and horseman and—some like to believe—an outlaw, too.

Those who only know about Cal Carrington through the romantic Wild West myths circulated in Jackson Hole find it hard to relate to him having had a more mundane life as a cattle drover, a wrangler and horse packer for the government, a Teton Valley rancher and farmer, or as a socialite and California snowbird. They don't want to hear about those parts of his life, provincially preferring to remember or think of him only as a reckless outlaw, regardless of whether or not it was true.

Henry and Rose Crabtree's son Hank, in an interview with biographer Ralph Martin, recalled: Cal was a "big, tall guy…built like Gary Cooper—tall, rangy, and slim. He looked the part, wore Western clothes the way they were meant to be worn." When he worked at the Bar BC dude ranch in Jackson Hole, there was a characterization by one of Cissy Patterson's biographers which pretty much summed it up: "Easterners photographed him to prove to their friends back home that the frontier still existed."[12]

There were four things Cal despised his entire life: his family, the Mormon church, Mormons in general, and sheep. "I had no use for sheep...wouldn't even wear woolen socks, or such trash as that."[13]

As we'll see, Cal never allowed his homesteading and farming activities in Teton Valley to tie him down. Grubbing out a homestead at Bates—in Idaho near Driggs—was only one of his many endeavors, sort of a hole card. He apparently didn't talk about it much during his early years in Jackson, but it, like his other ventures, ambitions, and skills, seasoned with a measure of good luck, all came together and paid off in spades over his lifetime.

In a recorded interview late in life, Cal did make one indisputable statement about himself, saying: "I always did like horses and women."[14]

The view from Harrups Hill when entering Teton Valley (undated).

4

Coming into the Tetons

In a sepia-toned scene out of the past, Cal, and a traveling companion, James H. Berger, trotted into Teton Basin, Idaho, in April 1897, on a rattling, light iron-tired wagon with four head of horses. The men wore Western work clothing common to the era consisting of overalls, blue denim shirts, boots, tall hats and loose neckerchiefs. Cal was about twenty-four years old at the time.[1]

Three of the four horses belonged to Cal, and as he told it years later, Jim had asked if he could come along with him. Berger was originally from Providence, Utah.[2] Although neither man could have articulated it, both were typical of the era, restlessly searching for something: new country, adventure, and livelihood, perhaps.

Cal and Jim had followed the old Mormon Trail, a muddy wagon road, from Cache Valley, Utah, where Cal had spent the winter. When asked some sixty years later in an interview, where he had been before then, he growled defensively, "That's none of your damn business," which has only added to the mystique of his early years.[3]

They were forced to hold over in Menan, Idaho, for nearly a month while the winter's accumulation of snow along the route to Teton Basin finally receded enough to get through.[4] They carried provisions with them, consisting of a sack of flour, dried apples and peaches, a container of honey and a ham.[5]

Rumors buzzed ahead of them in Teton Valley: "Look out for those two strangers, they're claim jumpers." Years later, in an interview, Cal still remonstrated angrily when recalling this malicious gossip.[6]

As early as 1889, Latter-day Saints in Salt Lake City had extolled the natural wonders and resources of Teton Valley in the *Desert News*, encouraging its settlement.[7] It's reasonable to assume that the two young men seeking to make a start had been influenced by those stories while living among Utah settlers.

Historian Fredrick Jackson declared the American frontier "finally closed" in 1892, five years before Cal's arrival in the Tetons, but conditions in the isolated high mountain valleys encompassing those mountains arguably didn't confirm that assessment. Surveyor William Owen described the country surrounding the Teton peaks that same year as "rugged and wild beyond the power of words to convey."[8]

Cal and Jim arrived in Teton Valley twenty years after its native inhabitants had been forcefully evicted to the Reservation, and only fourteen years after the Valley's first Mormon pioneers had arrived. It was the same year in which cattlemen announced sheep would not be permitted in Jackson Hole. Mountain man Beaver Dick Leigh who had once noted in his journal, "Teton Basin was the beautifulest sight in the whole world," was still living and guiding hunters there.[9]

But the springtime quagmire on frontier Driggs' Main Street was anything but "beautiful." It was a thoroughfare for large numbers of cattle, sheep and horses on the way to pasture. Melting snow, mud and manure combined to give it the mucky look of a "lazy man's barnyard." It was a springtime mien which characterized downtown Driggs and other frontier towns for decades.[10]

At Don Driggs' mercantile store, located in a homestead cabin, Cal purchased staples, including a year's supply of blackstrap molasses in a two and a half gallon can for $1.75. In the process, he questioned store owner Driggs about the prospects of homesteading in Teton Basin. A man named J. Moffat, who later served as a witness on Cal's Desert Entry submissions, overheard and advised Cal about an unclaimed tract at a place called Bates—named after Tom Bates, who had first taken up land there at the mouth of Mahogany Creek around 1888.[11]

Cal squatted (took up residence without title, as was the practice) on the 160-acre parcel, and according to BLM General Land Office (GLO) records, Berger settled a mile northwest, on a +159.64 acre parcel. A patent for the latter tract was issued under the Homestead Entry Act to James H. Berger on March 1, 1904.[12] What may not have been evident to Cal at the time was that the Bates area was sparsely settled for a reason—there were few streams and little readily available water.[13] Water rights and availability would be issues that were to plague him in later years.

Near the end of his life, in an interview, Cal was asked what he remembered most about coming into Teton Valley for the first time. No doubt the interviewer expected him to wax nostalgically about unsettled prairie or the rugged, snow-covered mountains, but men who engaged in the struggle of frontier existence rarely displayed such sentiment. Instead, Cal's reply echoed the simple pragmatism of the time: "The grass, grass everywhere, it was a damn good place to picket a horse."[14]

Earle F. Layser 53

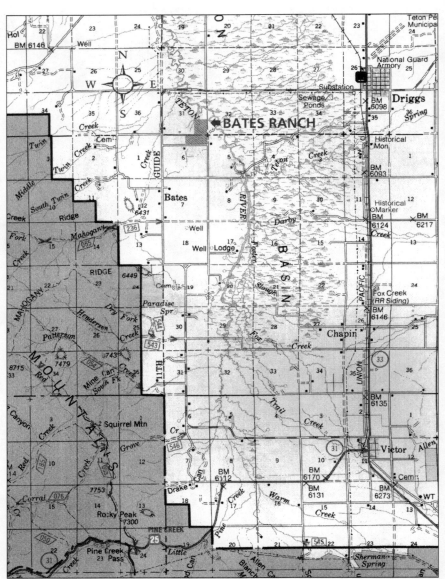

Map of the location of Cal's Bates Ranch in Teton Valley, Idaho.

5

Teton Valley Desert Land Entry

To locate the 160-acre Bates tract southwest of the Driggs settlement where Moffat directed him, Cal had to first ford the overflowing Teton River. Springtime crossing of the river in those days could be difficult; one ford was north of Bates, near Fox Creek.[1] The tract he finally located and "squatted on" ominously qualified as "desert land," meaning it was incapable of producing an agricultural crop without artificial irrigation. Anyone who wanted to take up the challenge of developing it through irrigation and successfully producing at least 80 acres of crop land within a four-year period could then purchase it from the government for $1.25 per acre under the 1877 Desert Land Act.

A bargain? Perhaps, but in practice it was not free land. Pioneering a farm and proving up required hard work, time,

NOTICE OF WATER RIGHT.

STATE OF IDAHO,
   County of Fremont } ss.

To All Concerned Notice is Hereby Given:

   1st. That George W Allen and Enoch Carrington
of Bates, Fremont Co., Idaho
hereby claim the use of the waters of The South Fork of Mohogany Creek
in Fremont County, Idaho
to the extent of Ten cubic feet per second.

   2nd. It is intended to divert said water at or near the point where a copy of this notice is posted, and more definitely described as follows: on the South Bank of the Main Channel of Mohogany Creek, at a point about 40 rods east of the NW Corner of the SW¼ of SW¼ Section 6, Twp 4 N R ¼5 E, B Meridian as previously claimed and recorded

(In above description give legal subdivision of land or describe the place with reference to some prominent landmark.)

   3rd. The purpose for which said water is intended to be used is
Agricultural and domestic use
The place of intended use is near Bates, Fremont County, Idaho

   4th. It is intended to divert said water by means of a reservoir to hold all of the high water of said South Mohogany Creek at a point for the Canyon about 1 mile above the headgate described in
~~The general course of the proposed canal is~~
The length of the proposed ~~canal~~ dam is for this reservoir is about 100 ft
It is intended to use said water for irrigating the following described land: NW¼ Section 5, NE¼ Sec 6, Twp 4 N, W½ SW¼ Section 32, E½ SE¼ Section 31, Twp 5 N R ¼5 E.

   5th. It is intended to have the works for diversion and use of said water as aforesaid completed within five years. (This must in no case exceed five years.)

Witness our hands at Bates Fremont Co., Idaho, this 29'
day of October 190 1.

George W Allen
Enoch Carrington

} Claimants

coping with adversity, and a rare item in those days, money.

Cal, with the help of neighbors, including probably Jim Berger, immediately set about building himself a stout cabin and shelter for his horses on the tract; establishing his claim and insuring himself the means to survive Teton Valley's brutal winter. He also set about putting up wild hay, cutting a supply of firewood and subsistence hunting. As Cal himself said, "There was plenty of hunting to keep a fellow alive." It probably didn't leave much time for anything else that first summer in 1897.

Topographically, Cal's Desert Entry parcel was on a bench west of the Teton River, with the eastern part being close to the river. But he had no way to raise water from it onto his land. Instead, in April 1897, he filed a water right claim to the "surplus water from John Holland's spring" near Horseshoe Creek. Later, in 1900 and 1901, he filed claims on water from Mahogany Creek. Establishing water rights and devloping irrigation for his land was a required step in the Desert Entry process. Cal's water right claims were recorded at Blackfoot, Idaho. Neighbors who recorded water rights from Mahogany Creek around the same time were early homesteaders George Allen, B. Dustin, and G.E. Stone.[2]

One year later, on June 5, 1901, Cal submitted a Declaration of Applicant at Oasis (near St. Anthony) in Fremont County, Idaho, providing his written testimony that the tract qualified as "desert land" and stating his intention to "reclaim" it. At this point he paid an application fee of fifteen dollars, plus twenty-five cents per acre. His application was identified on GLO records as "No. 3116."[3]

Earlier on the same day, he also filed a Declaration of Intention in St. Anthony, Idaho, stating under sworn oath, it was

Left: Enoch Carrington's and neighbor George Allen's
    1901 water right filing on Mahogany Creek.

DECLARATION OF INTENTION.

I, Enoch Carrington, do declare, on oath, that it is bona fide my intention to become a CITIZEN OF THE UNITED STATES OF AMERICA, and to renounce and abjure forever all allegiance and fidelity to all and any foreign Prince, Potentate, State and Sovereignty whatsoever, and particularly to the King of England of whom I was a subject.

Enoch Carrington

Sworn to and subscribed before me, at my office, this 5" day of June A. D. 189 1901.

A. M. Carter
Clerk of the District Court.

By Rae E. Davis
Deputy Clerk.

Fifth Judicial District Court in and for the State of Idaho.

Sworn 1901 statement by Enoch Carrington of intent to become a U.S. citizen.

his "...bona fide intention to become a citizen of the United States, and to renounce...forever all allegiance...to the King of England of whom he was a subject." A provision of the Desert Land Act required that the applicant be a citizen of the U.S. or to declare his intention of becoming one.[4]

During the years from 1900 to 1907, Cal doggedly submitted the required witness statements, various proofs, and underwent investigations of his labors and veracity, in order to prove up and gain title to his Bates tract. National Archive documents record a saga of Cal's persistent labors, trials and a share of tribulations: digging two miles of irrigation ditches with his neighbor Ed Seymour, clearing and grubbing fifty acres, building fence, planting twenty acres of timothy and oats, annually cutting wild hay, involvement in water right disputes, and traveling to Oasis, Blackfoot and St. Anthony, Idaho, to submit timely sworn and witnessed statements to the GLO.[5]

The application witnesses Cal employed in 1901, for example, included neighboring rancher Ed Seymour, rancher Carlos Moon, saloon keeper George Allen, rancher John H. Holland, and others residing at Oasis, Idaho. James Berger was also a witness on Cal's improvement affidavits in 1902.[6]

An aside: Cal's witness, John Holland, was a well known and controversial historical figure in early day Jackson Hole, one of the Hole's original settlers. At one time, it is suspected (but never proved) he may have lived on both sides of the law.

Holland originally had a homestead in Jackson Hole on Nowlin Creek (north of Miller's Butte) and also merchandised goods in Teton Valley and Jackson. Don Driggs' store was initially financed, at least in part, by Holland.[7] After Holland married Maude, Dan "Dad" Carpenter's youngest daughter,

In reply please refer to FHN   and date of this letter.

Address all communications to
"Director, U. S. Geological Survey,
Washington, D. C."

SUBJECT: Desert land entry.

DEPARTMENT OF THE INTERIOR
UNITED STATES GEOLOGICAL SURVEY
WASHINGTON, D. C.,

GBF

August 19, 1905.

Commissioner of the General Land Office,

      Washington, D.C.

Sir:

     Referring to your letters of January 19 and May 2, 1905, relative to D.L.E. No.3116, Enoch Carrington, lots 1 and 2, Sec.6, T.4 N., E½SE¼ Sec.31, T.5 N., R.45 E., Blackfoot, Idaho, land district, I have to state that from a field examination of this tract made July 5, 1905, it appears that while 20 acres have been prepared for irrigation, but about five acres have been actually irrigated and cultivated. It is believed that the water supply is insufficient and therefore recommendation is made that the case be specially examined by a representative of the General Land Office.

            Very respectfully,

                              H. C. Rizer

                     Acting Director.

Denial of Enoch Carrington's request
for Bates Desert Entry patent in 1905.

sometime in the late 1890s, he moved to Teton Basin. Carpenter was a Civil War veteran living in or near the Basin.

Cal boarded with and no doubt did ranch work for Holland during his early years in Jackson Hole.[8] Irrigation ditches that serve parts of the National Elk Refuge yet today are attributed to Holland. They were dug using horses and methods requiring a lot of labor. Cal's relationship with Holland is particularly relevant from the standpoint of horse rustling stories that later circulated and is further addressed in following chapters.

Cal submitted his final Desert Entry proof December 1904. And in August 1905, a full eight years from when he first saw the property, he made the final purchase payment of $160.29 (a dollar per acre) to the GLO in Blackfoot, Idaho. Some might care to speculate on how a foot-loose cowboy like Cal ever came up with $160.29. However, as we'll see, Cal had wrangled seasonal work with the Forest Service and Yellowstone National Park in those years, which paid cash money.

Taken at face value, all his labor, improvements, proofs, timely filings, and payments should have served to satisfy the cumbersome bureaucratic process, but there was a hitch. The Desert Land Act had a notorious history of producing fraudulent claims. According to the U. S. Bureau of Land Management, a majority of Desert Entry claims in the western U.S. were bogus.[9]

Claimants were inclined to fudge. With a wink and nod local witnesses went along with it. They were expected to be "credible," but the unstated code was: "you witness mine, I'll witness yours"—you scratch my back, I'll scratch yours. Together they were united by the land, labor and common destiny. It was a part of the culture, place, and time; the common man against the government. It fit a notion expressed in a popular 1850s song—*Uncle Sam is rich enough to give us all a farm...*

Not surprising then, but contrary to Cal's filed statements, in an August 1905 field inspection of his Bates tract, following the final proof submittal, an examiner noted: "...[only] twenty acres have been prepared for irrigation,...[and only] five acres have actually been irrigated and cultivated...[and further] it is believed the water supply is insufficient." As a consequence, it was recommended Carrington's case be "specially examined" by a GLO agent.

Patent was withheld pending the investigation.[10] It was, after all, understandably difficult to keep as many irons in the fire as Cal had going and still make his required improvements.

It was July 22, 1907, nearly two years later, before special agent Henry Brighton, from the GLO Field Division at Salt Lake City, traveled the two days, first by rail (the Oregon Short Line had reached Rexburg in 1899 and St. Anthony by 1902), and then by buckboard or saddle horse, to Bates in Teton Valley, to render his inspection and determination.

Inspector Brighton interviewed Teton Valley residents and neighbors J. Gale, J. Moffat, J. Black and B. Homer, all of whom vouched for Cal's veracity. Brighton determined the water rights, improvements, and water being run over the broken and previously cultivated land to be sufficient; although, he did remark on the uncertain fact that no crops were presently growing and Cal was nowhere to be found.[11] His neighbors covered for him, telling the inspector that Cal "was off working for the Forest Service." Brighton also noted, "The claim was improved with [a] fair log house and stable."

Cal Carrington's original 1897 Bates homestead cabin
as it appeared in 2004.
Photo by the author.

In his easygoing two-page report Brighton found in favor of
Cal, and in October 1907, it was recommended the claim go to
patent.[12] One consolation, at least Cal did not have to pay taxes
on the property for all the years he was waiting for patent
approval. Cal finally received title to the property ten years after
he had first taken up squatter's rights. It was granted by President
Theodore Roosevelt's authority October 26, 1907.

Still, it was nowhere near a record for time required to
gain a Desert Entry title. Early day Jackson Hole settler
John Cherry took nineteen years to prove up and receive his
Desert Land certificate at Willow Flat (today's Hatchet
Ranch) near Moran, Wyoming.[13] Willow Flat along the

Buffalo Fork has abundant natural water and was a curious desert entry claim, indeed.

However, there's much more to the story, Cal hadn't hung around tilling his land and fretting the outcome during all that time. While he managed to squeak by on the Desert Act requirements, work which totally occupied most men, he was actually simultaneously fully engaged elsewhere after the first year, as will become apparent. There was a reason GLO inspector Brighton couldn't find him on that day; Cal had also made a life in Jackson Hole, Yellowstone Park, and California during those ten years while proving up on his Desert Entry.

Cal was smart, ambitious and energetic. He hadn't put all his eggs into the Desert Entry basket, nor did he let any grass grow under his feet during those years. The truth is he actively pursued and successfully developed two separate and distinct lifestyles and personas: that of a Teton Valley homesteader and farmer and an adventuresome cowboy and wrangler in early day Jackson Hole and elsewhere.[14]

Right: Title for Cal's Bates property issued by the authority of Theodore Roosevelt in 1907.

THE UNITED STATES OF AMERICA

Desert Lands
Certificate No. 1494

)
)

To all to Whom these Presents shall Come——GREETING:

WHEREAS, Enoch Carrington

has deposited in the General Land Office of the United States a Certificate of the Register of the Land Office at

Blackfoot, Idaho   whereby it appears that full payment has been made

by the said Enoch Carrington

according to the provisions of the Act of Congress of the 24th of April, 1820, entitled, "An Act making further provisions for

the Sale of the Public Lands," and the acts supplemental thereto, for the

Lots one and two of section six intownship four north and the east half of

the south east quarter of section thirty one in township five north of range fofty

five east of the Boise Meridian, Idaho, containing one hundred sixty and twenty nine

hundredths acres.

according to the Official Plat of the Survey of the said Land, returned to the General Land Office by the Surveyor General,

which said Tract has been purchased by the saidEnoch Carrington

NOW, KNOW YE, That the United States of America, in consideration of the premises, and in conformity with the several Acts of Congress in such case made and provided, have GIVEN and GRANTED, and by these presents do GIVE and GRANT,

unto the said Enoch Carrington

and to his heirs, the said Tract above described.

TO HAVE AND TO HOLD the same, together with all the rights, privileges, immunities and appurtenances of whatsoever

nature thereunto belonging, unto the said Enoch Carrington

and to his heirs

and assigns forever, subject to any vested and accrued water rights for mining, agricultural, manufacturing or other purposes, and rights to ditches and reservoirs used in connection with such water rights, as may be recognized and acknowledged by the local customs, laws and decisions of Courts, and also subject to the right of the proprietor of a vein or lode, to extract and remove his ore therefrom, should the same be found to penetrate or intersect the premises hereby granted, as provided by law, and there is reserved from the lands hereby granted a right of way thereon for ditches or canals constructed by the authority of the United States.

IN TESTIMONY WHEREOF, I, **Theodore Roosevelt**   President of the United
States of America, have caused these letters to be made Patent, and the Seal of the General
Land Office to be hereunto affixed.

Given under my hand, at the City of Washington, the   twenty sixth

day of   October   , in the year of our Lord one thousand nine hundred

and   seven   , and of the Independence of the United States the one

hundred and thirty second

BY THE PRESIDENT: Theodore Roosevelt

By   F. M. McKean   Secretary.

Recorded   Vol. 677 Page 151   H. W. Sanford
                                                        Recorder of the General Land Office.
Transcribed from Book C of Patents, page 521, Fremont Co. Records.

6

Over the Mountains
into Early Day Jackson Hole

Cal first drifted across Teton Pass into Jackson Hole in 1898, the year after his arrival in Teton Valley and his having taken up squatter's rights on the Bates tract.[1] The pull Jackson Hole exerted on Cal was no less than destiny. In later years he put a colorful spin on it: "When I first rode into Jackson's Hole I didn't have nothin' but a long rope and an old buckskin horse."[2]

We can envision Cal riding his saddle horse, and leading a pack mare and extra mount, following an existing wagon road on the west side of the Teton River, along the foot of the Big Hole Mountains, toward the tiny Mormon settlement of Victor. The town had been platted in 1895 and named after Teton Valley mail carrier George Victor Sherwood.[3] By traveling along the west side of the river he avoided the springtime problem of fording the Teton River, although the route was still beset with swampy ground and tributary crossings.

Before heading out, Cal had put in a couple months work on his Bates place that spring; a necessary part of proving up and maintaining his Desert Entry claim and squatter's rights. Once that was accomplished though, it wasn't his style to just sit around watching wild hay grow.

Locating a wagon road going south, he proceeded from Victor up Trail Creek. It was early summer in the valley, but the rutted mountain road was steeped in mud and runoff, and rivulets flowed down the deep ruts. At higher elevation, he was required to dismount and lead his horses across snowbanks. Mormon settlers had improved the wagon track across the Pass in 1889 and again in 1893. Although wagon traffic was common by the 1890s, the road was still mostly impassable in the early muddy months.[4]

The whisperings Cal had heard about the Hole stoked his imagination; like a magnet the stories drew him across the Pass. At the 8431-foot-elevation summit it's likely he paused, gripped by views that had left trappers, explorers and early settlers before him agape, and countless others who have since followed.

Before him lay the astounding panoramic sweep of Jackson Hole, bisected by the pastel-green cottonwoods and meadows outlining the Snake River, bordered by vast drab green foothill prairies and buttes, behind all of which rose the Gros Ventre Mountains—Jackson Peak, Sleeping Indian, Crystal Mountain— with black-green forest and contrasting snow-capped summits. Breaths of mist magically appeared and disappeared as though the land was alive and breathing—a dramatic scene, which even today, remains among the West's most compelling.

On the Jackson Hole side, the wagon road descended steeply in a series of muddy, snow-filled, tight switchbacks to the base of the Pass where Elijah Nick Wilson and other Mormon settlers had raised a scattering of log cabins ten years earlier. When Cal returned along the same route at the end of summer, he would discover a newly built hotel, store and saloon at the foot of the Pass.[5]

At that time there was no town of Jackson. It didn't exist yet. The "Clubhouse" had been built in 1897, which served as a center for any community activities—dance hall, courtroom and commercial building. The next year Charles "Pap" Deloney would open his general store, around which a collection of buildings would begin to gather a few years later. It was a pivotal time in Jackson Hole's history; settlement was beginning in earnest throughout the Hole.[6]

At best it was an arduous, dawn-to-dark horseback trip from his Bates ranch to the west bank of the Snake River in those days. For wagons or buckboard, the Pass could be a two-day trip or more. Roadhouses would be constructed along the route in the following years. Undoubtedly Cal discovered a roiled Snake River, swollen with snowmelt and running too fast to ford or risk swimming his horse across. He probably camped on the riverbank, waiting for morning to cross by a crude ferry boat.

In those days the river was a major obstacle, effectively dividing the valley. It was only readily fordable during certain months of the year. Drownings were not an uncommon occurrence while attempting river crossings. One method used to get horses across the river in high water was to tie each horse to another's tail, then with a long lead rope, while riding the lead horse, swim them across. Another way was for a man to ride in the rear seat of a rowboat holding a long lead rope, while an oarsman paddled across. Either way, it was a risky business. Having to dodge driftwood made it even more hazardous.[7]

The first bridge at the Wilson crossing would not be constructed for another thirteen years, in 1911. In 1915 it washed out and a steel truss bridge was built. This bridge also washed out a few years later and yet again in the Kelly Flood of 1926.[8] The Wilson crossing continued to present problems

John Holland leading a pack horse with a bear hide, c 1900. *Courtesy of JHHSM, 1958.2814.001.*

for travelers and settlers into the 1920s. Menor's Ferry, twelve miles north as the raven flies, was the only other option for high-water crossings.

Over the years, going back and forth from his Teton Valley property to Jackson, we can be sure that Cal became intimately aware of the risky nature of both the Snake River and Teton Pass crossings. In an interview Cal said, "Never worried about the river. It had [braided smaller] channels. When we got to it, we crossed it."[9]

In those early years, Cal boarded with Dick Turpin and John Holland. He probably did ranch work for them, too. In his words, "I was around Bob Miller some, too."[10] These were some of Jackson Hole's original settlers, men with dubious reputations, who were tougher than rawhide and who had only recently morphed into "respectability." Cal knew and referred to them as the Hole's "oldtimers."[11]

Dick Turpin (aka William A. Swalley), a fiery, bushy-bearded pioneer, had moved to the Hole after it was rumored he'd killed a man. Turpin Meadow was named after him, but his original homestead was located immediately north of today's town of Jackson. Turpin also had a felonious assault charge brought against him in Jackson, which was dismissed by John Holland, the Hole's Justice of the Peace at the time.[12]

After Deloney opened his general store in 1899, Cal apparently boarded with Pap a time or two, also: "Living with Pap Deloney at that time the way I did, I lived as good as the rest of them...it cost me about ten dollars a month for groceries...a little pig meat, n' lard, flour n' syrup—goes a long ways, ya' know. Potatoes, canned goods—couldn't keep them from freezing."[13]

While it was never proven, Holland and Miller were suspected of providing outlaws with supplies during their earliest years in

Jackson Hole early settlers Dick Turpin (left)
and Frank Peterson, c 1905.
Courtesy of JHHSM, 1958.0340.001P.

Jackson Hole.[14] Holland was the posse leader at the infamous 1892 Cunningham Cabin shootout, where two alleged horse thieves were gunned down. Still, despite his rough reputation, Holland was the first bachelor settler ever to plant a garden in Jackson Hole. And he also carried mail across Teton Pass in winter.[15]

The Hole had earned a reputation as a hideout for horse thieves and outlaws in the 1880s and 1890s. As early as 1876, Lt. Gustavus Doane, on his epic winter trek through Jackson Hole, had reported, "It was a favorite rendezvous for desperadoes and thieves." Its 1890s residents were characterized by frontiersman Thomas E. Crawford (aka the Texas Kid), as: "homeless, reckless, straight-shooting and hard drinking." Crawford was also one of the citizen posse members at the 1892 Cunningham Cabin shootout.[16]

Historian Robert Betts points out that Western communities frequently prided themselves on their bad men, "a form of inverted civic pride."[17] Certainly, nowhere else was a reputation for badness more unequivocally celebrated than in early day Jackson Hole. But for whatever reason, in a 1957 interview, Cal was ambiguous on the subject: "I [didn't] know any real bad men. [But] I guess some weren't too nice in a way."[18]

Stories about Cal's early years in the Hole are colored by local lore and myths from that era. To put these in perspective, Cal had the life-long habit of being close-mouthed about some things, but conversely, he excelled at spinning yarns, a common practice of the times, essentially creating his own history. For those who badly want to believe the outlaw tales about him, this may be a disappointing revelation. Nonetheless, it may be comforting to learn that more factual accounts still contain a strong measure of Wild West melodrama.

Cal's reluctance to openly discuss his early years—which is particularly evident when historians interviewing him late in his life were told: "None of your damn business," or "Let's not talk about that,"[19]—was a survival habit learned from living in uncertain times and among men of questionable repute. The unspoken code to avoid altercations or trouble on the frontier was to say little and mind your own business.

Some have maintained, based on his taciturn behavior, name changes and later, his spinning of yarns, that Cal was hiding something; notably, involvement in organized livestock rustling. No doubt the intentional protection and boosting of Jackson Hole's Wild West image and myths for posterity enters into it, too—an unstated but commonly understood pact among the Hole's oldtimers and residents. They were the original "spin-doctors."

The incomplete story of Cal's early life in Jackson Hole and before he came into the Tetons has only served to bolster his mystique and stature in some circles. In his final years, he did loosen up somewhat, revealing parts of his life to friends, Teton Valley neighbors, and by giving two recorded interviews. Still, his early history is fragmentary, frequently based on hearsay, often contradictory, and blurred by time. It's been further confounded by Cal's own stories, which, while adding currency to his reputation, were sometimes contrived.

In the Western tradition for "stringing greeners," Cal, like many in that era, had a swaggering fondness for devilment; fabricating fanciful tales and embellishing stories for the benefit of those he considered greenhorns, pilgrims, tenderfeet, or dudes;

and also, especially for the ladies. Another euphemism for the practice was "stuffin' dudes."[20]

Cal's stories appear to have drawn upon and incorporated local historical events, yarns and scandals, as well as his own imagination and life experiences. To merely have secondhand knowledge of an event was enough to claim a personal association. Typically, he and others gave dudes what they wanted to hear, glamorous tales of lawless roguery and romance in which Cal generally played the starring role. He played to his audience.

Sometimes his tales were purposefully laced with subtle barbs, or were designed in an allegorical fashion, to vindicate or justify himself. Frequently, this was the case, for example, when he made references to his family. Author Nathaniel Burt characterized him as using few words, but those could be disdainfully mocking when he chose.[21] Jackson Hole oldtimer Charlie Peterson, Sr., amusedly recalled, "Cal was always trying to make a joke out of everything."[22]

Nevertheless, both true and cooked-up events have been equally passed along by journalists and in local folklore or otherwise handed down, making it difficult to distinguish between real happenings and contrived ones. For example, Cal apparently told Jackson hotel proprietress and member of the first ever all women Town Council, Rose Crabtree, "His mother was a cook in a lumber camp and had run off with some man and left him." Similarly, he confided to Cissy Patterson: "His mother had sold him to the captain of a ship sailing from England."[23] And in *Glass Houses*, Cissy wrote, "...his mother had deserted him, left him to wake up one morning crying alone in an upstairs room of a mining camp dance hall."

Two of Cissy's biographers recorded: "Cal had apprenticed to cattle rustlers and lived with Indian tribes; ...was in San Francisco during the 1906 earthquake;...had seen the inside of a jail; ...and had escaped a posse by plunging his horse into the ice-swollen Snake River as he clung to the horse's tail." And, another time, "A California sheriff started to close in on him for rustling..."[24] It all makes Hollywood seem tame!

However, there is no real evidence Cal ever did any jail time, nor lived with Indians. In fact, in a recorded interview when asked about Indians, Cal responded, "No, we had no Indians."[25]

Was Cal really in San Francisco on April 18, 1906? Possibly. He claimed he was, but there is no certain way to know. More likely, he was working near there in northern California for the Forest Service at the time.[26] The possibility that he was there adds glamour to his image, though.

Did he really apprentice to cattle rustlers and escape a posse by holding on to his swimming horse's tail in an ice-swollen river? That Cal worked for, or was "apprenticed to," men who may have once been outlaws is true, but his work for them appears to have been wrangling or ranching, not rustling. Swimming an ice-swollen river with posse in pursuit is a tall tale, amusing for its outrageousness.

Less dramatic, but more to the facts regarding river crossings, author Struthers Burt wrote: "There wasn't a river Cal wouldn't swim on a horse, although he never learned to swim himself."[27]

You can be certain Cal had better sense than to try to swim the ice-swollen Snake River, by horse or otherwise. And did he ever have a posse pursue him for rustling? Anytime a posse was assembled in the old West, it generally made headlines in local newspapers—as did, for that matter, the capture of outlaws—in reference to the tale that, "all the outlaws in his gang were captured except Cal." But no

Jackson Hole posse is known to have been assembled fitting the time period, nor any outlaw captures recorded.

The most persistent rumor circulated about Cal, but unsubstantiated, is that when he first came into the Hole he was an outlaw, a horse thief. Author and rancher Struthers Burt wrote, when he first met Cal, "He had a reputation for badness." Burt was warned: "He'd steal the rope off my saddle—while I was looking, too."[28]

This type of hearsay continues to be passed along to this day. As recent as 2003, award-winning author J. Huyler claimed, "[Cal] was hiding from his past... that's why he changed his name."[29] Yet Cal's playing with his name, as was shown earlier, had nothing to do with hiding from an outlaw past. It was directed at his family.

In later years, Cal entertained himself by perpetuating the horse thief rumors and playing up his outlaw reputation. Jackson buzz to this day still has it that, "He and his gang hid stolen horses in Flat Creek Canyon, where they would change the brands."[30]

Flat Creek Ranch owner Cissy Patterson amused herself by playing along with and contributing to the outrageous tales, explaining: "Flat Creek Canyon was ideal for hiding his stolen horses." And Cal is frequently quoted as having said, "In Flat Creek Canyon, I can spot the sheriff a-comin' or a-goin'."[31]

Local historian W. Gillette popularized it, too, writing: "A horse thieving ring was established among Cal and five other men..." Two of these men Gillette identified as proven horse thieves Ed Harrington (aka Ed Trafton, the Yellowstone National Park "gentleman bandit") and Teton Valley's Lum Nickerson. Cal, and these men, according to Gillette, drove the stolen horses across Owen Wister's "horse thief trail" and used Cal's Flat Creek Ranch in Jackson Hole to change the brands, after which they would take the stolen horses over the Continental Divide to sell to unsuspecting buyers.[32] Jackson's hotel proprietress, Rose Crabtree, who was said to be as "sharp as a whip," passed the yarn along too, saying: "Cal belonged to a gang of six rustlers, all the men were caught except Cal."[33]

However, those stories simply don't add up chronologically, as we'll see. For example, Cal didn't have or own the Flat Creek Ranch yet in those years—it didn't exist—and Harrington and Nickerson had been busted for stealing horses long before, in 1887.

In truth, Cal arrived in Jackson Hole after those reckless times, some years after the last hoorah for organized horse thievery and the time when the Hole had earned its outlaw reputation. Ruthless efforts in 1893 by Montana stock growers and their paid regulators had dealt out harsh discouragement and abruptly brought an end to any organized rustling in and about the area.[34]

Cal's arrival in the Hole, however, was close on the heels of the outlaw era, and some suspected and known rustlers who hadn't been sent to the great roundup in the sky were unquestionably still around. Wisely, they were no longer engaged in the pre-owned horse business. But the outlaw times and events were still fresh in the memory and lives of Jackson Hole's populace.

Still, to fully address and resolve the recurrent question of what Cal's involvement, if any, may have been with organized horse rustling, those times and the back-fence lore deserve additional examination. Folk tales, for example, still circulate today about his involvement with an outlaw "gang of six," the "red bandana gang," and the "Jackson Hole brotherhood."[35] What actually were these organizations and, if they really ever did exist, what was their purpose?

7

Wild West Tales

An example demonstrating how bogus tales were concocted and passed along in those times was the outlaw Ed Harrington's fondness for telling all those who cared to listen that Owen Wister patterned his character the Virginian after him—most believed it was the villain Trampas instead.[1]

After a lifetime as a desperado and thief, Harrington ironically died of natural causes in a Los Angeles ice cream parlor in 1922. He had gone to California with a fabricated story in his pocket to sell to the Hollywood movie industry. The *Los Angeles Times* ran the headlines: *"'The Virginian' Dies Suddenly—Owen Wister Novel Hero Was Real Pioneer—Blazed First Trails Into Jackson Hole Country..."*[2]

Harrington wasn't alone among the Virginian wannabes.

Thomas Crawford, the "Texas Kid," also claimed "he could name the boy who was the Virginian,"[3] but he never did divulge just who he thought it might be.

Playing with the truth was not limited to a nefarious few back then. A 1914 investigator, E.N. Moody, assigned to look into a questionable Jackson event, became thoroughly frustrated by the wild stories he was told. Moody complained, "... all the townspeople had a compulsion to outdo a character named John Cherry, who excelled in telling tall tales."[4]

John Cherry came into the Hole in 1887. He had a homestead at Warm Springs north of Kelly, and a Desert Entry tract near Moran that later became known as the Hatchet Ranch. Cherry, who also became a hunting guide and dude wrangler, was notoriously careless with the truth, earning a reputation for telling exaggerated tales and falsehoods. He claimed Doc Middleton, the infamous Nebraska horse thief, was his brother.[5]

Retelling and reinventing versions of early day episodes, and the impromptu substitution of main characters, kept the glamour of the Wild West glowing. It also helped to perpetuate Jackson's reputation as a rowdy place populated with bad men and outlaws, a tough, fearless, and heroic image Jackson Holers liked to identify with and took serious pride in maintaining. After all, "stuffin' dudes" was great entertainment.

Already, at the turn of the twentieth century, the glamour of a Wild West reputation helped spur the tourist economy. By 1897, Jackson Hole was known as a mountain resort and was serving sportsmen and tourists.[6] But outrageous Wild West tales served another purpose, too, that of distracting attention from those who may have actually had a disreputable past to hide. It made it difficult to tell just who the outlaws really were or had ever been.

There should not be any doubt that Cal would have been acquainted with Ed Harrington and his ilk, the Cunningham Cabin incident, and other outlaw lore, especially after living and working among the Hole's oldtimers. Everyone in Teton Valley and Jackson Hole must have been familiar with the traditional outlaw wisdom in those days. Still, when he was asked in an interview about a fellow by the name of Teton Jackson, Cal gave a curious reply: "I don't believe he was much of anything. I don't believe much in things like that." Asked if he had known him, Cal replied: "The old Teton Jackson I never saw. He was there... before I was."[7]

Regardless, Cissy Patterson's biographers and others, to this day continue to perpetuate the myth: "Cal belonged to a 'gang of six' rustlers, identified by the red bandanas they wore...only Cal was never caught."[8] However, Cal could not have been part of the so called gang of six, as will become evident, and a red bandana wasn't an identification for organized rustlers, it was the badge of the "Jackson Hole brotherhood," which we'll also explain.[9]

The Gang of Six

Looking back to early times when winter closed the mountain passes into the Hole, it afforded a snowbound hideaway for scoundrels wanting to evade the law. In winter no one could get in or out of the valley.

In 1885, only seven men wintered inside the Hole.[10] They were a scruffy bunch, unshaven and rank, overalls torn and patched, denim shirts ragged, neckerchiefs filthy, mackinaws blackened from campfire smoke, soot and dirt, and their boots were near worn out. None of them had any cash money, and legitimate prospects to rectify that situation were slim to none.

There were plenty of reasons to be suspicious of these men. Earlier that autumn, a posse led by Pap Conant had searched the Hole. Whisperings had it that a herd of steers which had mysteriously vanished from the Wind River country was hidden there. Pap and his riders found "a great many horse sign," including two bands of ponies of unknown ownership, one grazing on Flat Creek Meadows and another corralled in Leek's Draw.[11] The posse took no action, but federal marshals were interested to learn what they had found.

When spring brought the seven to the surface, federal marshals somehow corralled one of them, Bill Arnn, and brought him in for an official chat. (This is not the same Arnn who rode with Butch Cassidy's gang.)

The origin of a rumored "gang of six" likely arises from a sworn statement given by William Arnn, wherein he testified to federal marshals at Malad, Idaho—who were investigating a suspicion that rustlers were using Jackson Hole for a winter hideout—that: "...just six men, besides himself, had spent the winter in the Hole." They were John Holland, Bob Miller, Bill Thompson and his partner Hilderbrand, Lock Bye and Ed Harrington.[12]

Harrington (aka Ed Trafton) was a renowned thief and had already done time for rustling. Thompson and his partner, Hilderbrand, were compadres of the notorious outlaw Teton Jackson (aka William Bradford, Harvey Gleason, et al). John Holland, Bob Miller and the others were suspect by association. There's also some evidence Holland and Miller were providing supplies for the outlaws.[13] Teton Jackson himself was, at the time, cooling off in the Boise Penitentiary for grand larceny; a fancy way of saying "horse stealing."

Presumably, Arnn's testimony regarding the presence of six miscreants who overwintered in the Hole constitutes the origin for back fence references to a shadowy gang of six in the years afterward.[14] But the "gang of six" was years before Cal's time.

Red Bandana Gang and the Brotherhood

A few years later, in 1887, Teton Valley ranchers got fed up with having their livestock disappear. Hiram Lapham, the first settler in Teton Valley, led a posse that caught up with Ed Harrington, Lum Nickerson, and Jim Robertson in eastern Idaho, while they were engaged in rounding up ponies that didn't belong to them. They were taking the stolen horses across the Tetons, by way of Conant Pass into Jackson Hole, where they'd alter the brands and then sell the stock to unsuspecting buyers. In the donnybrook that followed, Jim was shot and died, and Lum and Ed were sent to the local slammer. In a failed escape attempt by the outlaws, Ed was shot in the foot and graduated to four years at Leavenworth.[15]

Owen Wister's material for *The Virginian*, published in 1902, is believed to be based, in part, on those happenings. The old Indian trail across the Tetons at Conant Pass (actually today's Jackass Pass) was Wister's "horse thief trail." Wister captured imaginations everywhere by penning: "...somewhere at the eastern base of the Tetons did those hoof prints disappear into a mountain sanctuary where many crooked paths have led."[16]

However, again, those outlaw events took place long before Carrington arrived in Teton Valley or Jackson Hole. Likewise, the 1892 Jackson Hole Cunningham Cabin shootout with alleged horse thieves was before Cal's time, as was the capture of Butch Cassidy in Star Valley earlier that same year, the capture of Sylvester Summers at Wolverine, Idaho, and Jack Bliss and Kid Collier in Uinta County, Wyoming—all apprehended by range detectives and/or Montana stockmen's paid regulators,[17] who were determined, once and for all, to rid the range of rustling.

The notorious outlaw activities of Teton Jackson (aka Harvey Gleason, William Bradford, et al) and his first lieutenant Bill "Red" Thompson were even before those events. Teton went to jail in 1885 for horse rustling, then escaped and returned to Jackson Hole. He was recaptured and jailed again and eventually moved on to Lander after selling his Jackson "fortress" (log buildings and squatter's right claim) to Robert Miller sometime after 1885.[19]

Ironically, some of the Jackson Hole posse members involved in the murky Cunningham Cabin incident were themselves rumored to have been involved with or associated with livestock rustlers at times. And the federal marshals who enlisted the Jackson posse members were later believed to be imposters— hired Montana stockmen regulators. Jackson's John Holland had been appointed, without proper authority, to lead a posse of local citizenry whose family names today are respected as among the Hole's earliest pioneers.[20]

It is essential to understanding Jackson Hole's early history, and the many contradictory tales surrounding events, to know that the Cunningham Cabin episode resulted in purposeful muddling of the facts by participants and Jackson's citizenry right up until very recent times.

After the Cunningham shootout, when the Jackson posse members had time to reconsider their headlong involvement and killing of two alleged outlaws, they feared possible retribution from both the law and outlaws. The participants became understandably closemouthed about the whole incident. In self-interest, they cloaked the happening in a brotherhood of silence, purposely obfuscating the whole affair with wild and conflicting tales. Settler and posse member Mose Giltner pretty much summed up the feelings for all of them afterward, saying: "He [Giltner] was a damn fool to have ever gotten involved."[21]

Meanwhile, the *Cheyenne Tribune* lauded Holland as "the embodiment of law and order," adding, "The impression that Jackson's Hole is peopled by rustlers and thieves is erroneous...their good names should not be sullied by classing them with thieves, rustlers and regulators,"[22] commentary that no doubt made Jackson Holers shuffle nervously and self-consciously glance sideways to see the reaction of the men beside them.

The Jackson Hole brotherhood proved successful in covering up and keeping a lid on things. Everyone, it seemed, embellished a different version of the Cunningham incident. The event's history is comprised of conflicting and inconsistent stories. Early day incidents and events up to 1892 had justifiably given Jackson Hole a reputation for being an outlaw hideout. After that, history was purposefully confounded by a cautious and worried citizenry's cover-up, distortions and imaginative retellings designed to protect themselves and to "string greeners." Behind it all was the pact of the so-called brotherhood that self-servingly protected the early settlers who had participated in the Cunningham Cabin affair.

Because of the historical vagueness and mystery surrounding the brotherhood, it has sometimes been mistakenly assumed to have been connected with organized rustling. This was not the case. However, the brotherhood was comprised of the Hole's original settlers, some of whom Cal hung around or found employment with, and it was a notable presence when he first rode into the Hole.

In a 1957 interview, and in an unusual lapse of guardedness, Cal disclosed the key for this early day Jackson Hole enigma, stating: "The red bandana gang was a brotherhood of oldtimers, who banded together to do what they wanted to do... they all went together...They all had a red squaw bandana for a badge...If you saw a man in the country riding around without a red bandana, you knew he was a stranger." Significantly, he then added, "They quit wearing them the year after I hit Jackson [in 1899]."[23]

The brotherhood and red bandana gang were one and the same. Their origin is presumably attributed to the Cunningham Cabin incident cover up, not rustling. They originated in the self-serving interest of protecting the Cunningham Cabin shootout participants, and evolved to include covering up any mountain law (vigilance committee) activities, shady doings, and dubious reputations, in general.

In an interview, Cal played down Jackson's outlaw reputation saying: "Well, I heard more stories [about outlaws] outside Jackson than I did in. When I got to Jackson, they all said the ones told me them stories was damn liars... then they told me what [really] happened."[24] Unfortunately, there it was dropped. He was not asked to explain what he thought "really did happen," nor did Cal further volunteer his knowledge.

This is not to say that Jackson Hole wasn't a rowdy, uproarious place back then—it was. And if a tourist had asked an oldtimer where all the outlaws went, he may have gotten a knowing wink with the wry reply: "We're all still here, partner."

One must conclude the days of organized horse rustling activities in and about Jackson Hole and Teton Valley pretty much took place before Carrington's arrival. Montana stockgrowers had ruthlessly put an abrupt end to those shenanigans in the early 1890s, swearing to rid the range of the rustling scourge once and for all. They effectively made the penalty for stealing livestock so severe that the pre-owned horse business lost any attractions. Any noteworthy outlaw episodes after that would certainly have been recorded by historians and journalists, but none were.[25]

8

Government Horse Packer
and
Forest Ranger

If Cal wasn't stealing livestock or riding with outlaws in those early years in Jackson Hole, as has been popularized, just what was he doing—besides spending time with and doing ranch work for some pretty rough customers in the Hole and grubbing out a homestead in Teton Valley?

As it turns out, for the period after he first came into the Hole—from around 1898-1908—Cal worked seasonally as a wrangler and horse packer for Yellowstone National Park and the Yellowstone Forest Reserve, and as a forest ranger for the Teton National Forest. He also worked for the Forest Service in northern California from 1906 to 1908.[1] Carrington's neighbors in Teton Valley had informed the GLO Desert Land Entry Inspector, Brighton, correctly in 1906 Cal "was off working for the Forest Service."[2]

How do we know this? After all, it conflicts with popular lore that Cal was involved in horse rustling during the time. In 1957, Jackson Hole rancher Cliff Hansen, who was also a member of the University of Wyoming Board of Trustees at the time, hauled Cal over to the history department at Laramie for a recorded interview. Somehow Cliff overcame Cal's usual reticence; perhaps Cliff knew the right questions to ask. In any case, Cal, at age eighty four, waxed loquaciously and entertainingly—albeit disjointedly—on subjects he had never spilled the beans on before. Conversely, a year later he refused to answer similar questions with another interviewer in Teton Valley.[3]

"In 1898-1899, somewhere along there," Cal recollected, "I packed the surveyors on the Lamar River out to Yancy's old stage station [at Tower Falls] ...and then over to the Canyon Hotel."[4] This may have been Arnold Hague's U.S. Geological Survey party, or perhaps one of Hiram Chittenden's survey crews. More likely, in the Lamar it was the former.

The 2.1-million-acre Yellowstone National Park was established in 1872 under President Ulysses S. Grant's authority. The National Park Service came into being in 1916; until then, the park was under the command of the U.S. Army. Cal began working for the infant Yellowstone National Park while it was still administered by the Army.

Cal described it as his first time in Yellowstone National Park. Where he got the horses to do the packing and how he got the job he didn't say. Generally, horse packers in those days were expected to provide their own outfit and pack animals, but it's possible he may have had use of some government stock, too. Cal recalled, "Once at Norris, sleeping in a soldier's camp on a moonlight night, [I] woke up. A bear was standing at the foot of the bed. Scared us both. [But] he went away."[5]

Cal claimed, "Coming down out of the Park with my pack outfit...I overtook Beaver Tooth Dick [Leigh]—first time I met him. He was a different character.

" 'Have a drink,' Beaver Tooth said.

" 'Yeah', and I took a drink.

" 'Got me another bottle here.'

" 'How much you want for it?'

" 'Dollar.' "

Cal said, "I gave him a dollar. And that night I thought I'd take a drink before I ate and it was nothing but tea. That was my first introduction to old Beaver Tooth."[6]

On the way out, or way in the next summer, Cal, by chance, met Colonel A.A. Anderson, Superintendent of Forest Reserves (not George S. Anderson, Military Superintendent of Yellowstone, who saved the Park's bison from poachers), who was camped at the old Yellowstone Station, today's South Entrance.[7]

"He [Anderson] wanted me. But I told him I was going to work [up in the Park] for Chittenden."[8]

Hiram Chittenden is credited with having designed the road system in Yellowstone, and having engineered other enduring structures, such as the Gardiner entrance gate, around this time period. He also launched a career as a historian by writing an 1895 history of Yellowstone Park.)

"Anderson said, 'I'll fix it up.'

"And off he went," according to Cal. "Sure enough, next morning I was transferred into the Forest Service."

Cal presumably was recruited as a wrangler and packer for Colonel Anderson's monumental survey of the boundary of the Yellowstone Forest Reserve–a vast tract of forest and mountainous land encompassing 8,829,000 acres surrounding Yellowstone National Park. It took a party of ten men with thirty-five saddle and pack horses over three months, moving camp almost everyday, to accomplish the job. It was a feat that is unimaginable today. [9]

Carrington went back and forth between wrangling and horse packing for the Park and Forest Service and working his property in Bates in those years. The trip across The Pass was still, at best, an all day endurance affair back then. Jackson Holers referred to the trip to Victor as "going outside."

September 18-19, 1900, Theodore Roosevelt came through Rexburg on his vice presidential campaign. "At that time," Cal says, "John Holland, the oldtimer from Jackson, was living in the [Teton] Basin and I was breaking broncs for him. [10]" "Holland and I rode down to Rexburg—that's thirty-five miles; and I was going to ride a bronc [for Roosevelt]... when I got down there the bronc wouldn't switch its tail. The crowd was so thick the horse was scared to death. So I got out of a big chore." [11] As an afterthought, Cal added, "He [Roosevelt] was a nice ol' fella. I liked him...Teddy done more for our whole Western country than any president ever done." [12]

Anderson divided the vast Yellowstone Forest Reserve into four divisions. Robert Miller was appointed supervisor of the Teton Division from 1902 to 1908. It included most of the mountains and forests surrounding Jackson Hole. W.C. "Pap" Deloney had held the first supervisor post until 1902, when he resigned. Deloney hired the first crews ever for fire suppression in the Jackson Hole area for the Forty-Mile Fire in the Hoback in 1900. [13]

Local communities generally supported the role of the Forest Service in those early years.

Cal recalled, "I come down from the Park after surveying was done and Bob Miller put me... down on Porcupine [Creek, south of Jackson] to fight forest fire."[14] Next, "Miller sent me down to Star Valley... when they made that drive, the Wind River Rangers and them from Pinedale [Bridger Division.] In fact there was twenty-two of us in camp on Cottonwood [Creek]...and the sheep was on Piney [Creek]...Covey put his sheep right through, didn't pay any attention to the ranger... So we goes up there [with Anderson] and drives them off the Reserve."[15]

In those years, it was the practice of some sheepmen to burn the forest to create more area for sheep grazing. Large numbers of sheep were being brought in by owners from Utah and they were consuming the forage local farmers' livestock might otherwise utilize. They were none too fondly called "transient sheep." Sometime around 1905, sixty thousand transient sheep with forty armed herders were put into the Forest Reserve by four large owners out of Utah.[16]

Anderson gathered all his rangers—about sixty-five—in full regalia, armed and mounted. He told them, "I propose to remove the herders and their flocks from the Reserve using whatever force necessary... every man who is willing to do this take one step forward." Every man stepped forward, and Anderson was told, "Superintendent, there isn't a man here who wouldn't follow you plumb to hell."[17] Cal, we can presume, was among those men.

The rangers confronted the sheepmen, and then forming a line of horsemen behind the sheep, gathered them up and drove them to the eastern boundary of the Reserve. Meanwhile, an injunction was obtained restraining them from reentering the

Reserve. The sheep were caught between the Reserve and irate Green River cattlemen.

"A couple days later," Cal said, "an accident happened to the sheep." The cattlemen killed eight hundred sheep and burned the herder's outfits. "Covey [the sheepman] cried like a kid. I was in camp. I seen that," Cal remembered. "They [Anderson] let him take the sheep back over the Reserve, so he would have some left."[18]

The wild and, literally, woolly incident Cal refers to was a historically significant one in the management of National Forest ranges. Moreover, before it was finished the authority for the Forest Service to regulate livestock operators and require grazing permits was firmly established by the courts.

Both his Desert Entry application and Forest Service employment required that Cal become a U.S. citizen. In June 1901, he had entered a Declaration of Intention to become a citizen of the U.S. at the Fifth Judicial District, Fremont County, Idaho, and, in June 1905, because of lapsed time, he executed another similar sworn statement declaring intention to become a citizen. On February 10, 1905, he returned to the Fifth District Court and finally became a naturalized citizen, swearing before a court clerk that he had "behaved as a man of good moral character...since emigrating from England."[19]

Following his naturalization, and continuing his string of Park and Forest Service jobs, Cal was appointed as an Assistant Forest Ranger in July 1, 1905, for the Teton Division of the Yellowstone Forest Reserve at sixty dollars a month, a seasonal job back then.[20] In any case, it was certainly easier, at least in some ways, and steadier than seasonal ranch work. Most important, it paid a salary.

Back then it was generally the practice for the forest service to find the most respected, toughest, no-nonsense person in the local community to appoint as ranger or forest supervisor. In those days the Forest Service was an agency with a mission. One ranger expressed it this way: "It was a wonderful thing to have a government bureau with nothing but young men in it. There was no sign of inertia or red-tape inhibitions."

The cabin where Robert Miller conducted his Forest Service administrative duties is still standing at the Miller Ranch historical site on the National Elk Refuge today.

The first rangers, like Cal, were hired for their skills as wranglers and packers rather than professional forestry or range management. One of the requirements a prospective ranger had to fulfill before he got the job was a practical examination which included packing a horse. The test was conducted from the Miller barn located behind their log house. A candidate ranger would mount his saddle horse and leading the horse he had been required to pack, lope out and back for a mile or so. If the pack stayed on he passed the exam. In Cal's case, where Miller was personally acquainted with his capabilities, the formality of any exam may have been waived, or at most, conducted in half-serious fun.

Cal and others already had a tradition set by Roland W. Brown, the first forest ranger in the Teton region. Brown held the job from 1898-1910, and his duties covered both Jackson Hole and Teton Valley.[21] Carrington claimed Brown was "fired," but in reality Brown was reassigned to Teton Basin when the Reserve was reorganized. Rudolph "Rosie" Rosencrans was another well-known, early-day ranger who worked in the Teton Division beginning in 1904. "Rosie's Ridge," north of Blackrock Creek along Wyoming state highway 26/287, is named after

1318.

United States

Department of Agriculture,

Washington, D. C., June 28, 1905.

Mr. ENOCH CARRINGTON - - - - - - - - - - - - - - - - - , of the State of WYOMING - , is hereby appointed

Assistant Forest Ranger,

In the Forest Service,

in the United States Department of Agriculture, at a salary at the rate of Seven Hundred and Twenty ($720.00) Dollars per annum, on the miscellaneous roll, paid from the fund appropriated for "General Expenses, Forest Service."

By transfer from a Ranger at $60.00 per month, on the roll paid from the fund appropriated for the "Protection of Forest Reserves, 1905," assigned to the Bureau of Forestry.

The above-named appointee is hereby required to report for duty in writing, to the Forester, Chief of the Forest Service, and be subject to the rules and orders of the Secretary of Agriculture. This appointment shall take effect on July 1, 1905.

James Wilson
Secretary of Agriculture.

him. After a long career, Rosie retired due to failing eyesight. He declined corrective surgery, saying, "I have seen enough beauty for a lifetime."[22]

In those days, rangers were solitary, side-armed horsemen whose job entailed regulation of grazing and timber cutting on the Forest Reserves. They were also expected to enforce the game laws where they existed. Cal, however, like most at the time, did not hunt by the calendar. Jackson Hole settlers subsisted on game meat year round.

Cal has been quoted as saying: "The government had no business telling a man what to do in his own mountains."[23] That would appear to be an attitude in conflict with his ranger duties. But on the other hand, Cal's mindset wouldn't have applied universally. This was the era of the elk tuskers and Cal, like other rangers and wardens at the time, had strong support from the local populace. The tuskers killed elk only for their eye teeth or "ivories," which they then sold, leaving the rest of the animal to rot. Jackson Holers were rightfully angry about the wanton slaughtering of elk, which they relied on for subsistence. They finally formed a vigilance committee in 1906 and issued the tuskers a mountain law ultimatum, "clear out or be shot."[24]

Forest Reserve Superintendent A.A. Anderson learned firsthand of the difficulty of enforcing the game laws. He met a young man on the trail who had an out-of-season deer tied on his pack horse and arrested him. At the trial a six-man jury

Left: USDA Forest Service 1905 certificate of appointment
   to Assistant Forest Ranger.

deliberated briefly and returned their verdict: "He did it, but we won't find him guilty this time."[25]

In 1905, Cal was undoubtedly discouraged and angry about the GLO examiner's denial of his Bates Desert Entry final approval. A year passed and it still hung fire, awaiting the government's investigation. Cal wouldn't actually learn of its approval until the autumn of 1907.[26] In the meanwhile, he found employment with the Forest Service in northern California. Two of Cissy's biographers put Cal in San Francisco on April 18, 1906, during the great earthquake, and it's likely he was nearby.[27] Cal's extended absence from Teton Valley around this time period is verified by GLO Inspector Brighton's July 22, 1907 report: "I did not see the claimant. He is said to be in the U.S. Forestry Service and has been for a year or more so employed."[28]

"I couldn't work under Miller," Cal said, "I didn't like him. He wanted me to work with his cows and I didn't want cows no more. I got outta that...I got transferred thru Pinchot [Chief of the Forest Service] to California...I was down there [in California] for two seasons and then I came home and went guiding [dudes and hunters.]"[29]

In contrast, illustrating how hearsay from remarks—no doubt originally made in jest— followed Cal around, in 1979 Cissy Patterson's biographer Ralph Martin described the circumstances under which Cal left California in this manner: "Rustling horses had become his business until a California sheriff started to close in on him. Cal then took a packhorse named Quincy and made the long trek across the West to Jackson."[30]

Cal could have made the long horseback ride from California to Jackson (actually he probably first returned to Teton Valley) leading his packhorse named Quincy. It's a romantic image. On the other hand, more likely he made use of the railroad to get himself and his horses home. And it's very unlikely a sheriff was closing in on him for rustling while he was working for the Forest Service. He probably named his packhorse Quincy after the town where he was stationed with the Forest Service.

It's reasonable to assume Cal came home from California because he received word that he had finally gotten title to his Bates Ranch[31] and, for the reason he stated in his 1957 interview, to guide dudes and hunters with John Holland.

The town of Jackson, Wyoming, in 1907.
Courtesy of JHHSM, 1958.0225.001P.

9

Rustling Up a Living
in
Early Day Jackson Hole

Jackson Hole underwent radical transformation in the latter part of the nineteenth century as nesters and tourists began pouring in. In 1890, the year Wyoming Territory became a state, sixty-four people were reportedly living in the Hole. But by the 1900 census the Hole had undergone cinch-busting growth from a sparsely settled frontier valley to having one hundred forty-five farms and mountain ranches, along with five post offices.[1] Cal had arrived in the Hole just as this rapid change was taking place. It was the end of one era, and beginning of a new.

Beaver Dick Leigh, the mountain man who had guided the Hayden Survey, died in 1899, and was buried on a bluff near Rexburg, Idaho, viewing the distant Tetons. His death at the turn of the century also marked the end of an earlier time.[2]

By the turn of the twentieth century, sixty-five homesteads had been taken up just within the area that is now the southern end of the National Elk Refuge. The naturally occurring marshes and springs there—referred to as "the swamp" or "morass," the place where not long before Teton Jackson and his outlaw gang had stood off lawmen— provided settlers with plenty of "slough-grass" hay for their livestock; while the landmark prominence, once known as Carnes' Butte, became known as Miller's Butte to the newcomers.

Although it was suspected that early settlers John Carnes, John Holland and Bob Miller had been accomplices in pre-owned horse dealings, and were in earlier times providing supplies for outlaws in the Hole, it was never proven. Maybe they had just been neighborly, since their original homesteads were located next or near to Teton Jackson's gang's fortress in "the morass."

As times changed, those men sought to divert attention away from their shady pasts, metamorphosing into Jackson Hole's most reputable, prosperous and entitled citizenry as ranchers, a banker, mail carrier, constable, justice of the peace, U.S. commissioner and even a national forest supervisor.

Some, however, failed to graduate from the outlaw line of work. Harrington ended up in and out of jail, as did Teton Jackson, before both eventually became "respectable." Thompson, meanwhile, just faded from the scene.

Insight into the shenanigans involved in the startup of early day ranches was provided by Pap Conant's posse's 1885 foray into the Hole in search of stolen cattle and their finding steers at the head of Spread Creek and horses hidden elsewhere.[3]

Cal also revealed years later in an interview how certain enterprising hooligans got their ranching starts: "They picked up cattle off the Green River trail... [and] drove them back up here...'Course they'd be some horses and whenever they got a stray...they pushed him in here [too]."[4]

But, again, all this was before Cal's time. John Holland and John Carnes obviously knew the Bacon Creek-Gros Ventre trail from the Green River into Jackson Hole. They are credited with being the first to bring a wagon and farm equipment into the Hole using that route.[5]

However, most agree, cattle rustling never amounted to much in Jackson Hole, because cows were generally too slow moving to be brought in and out of the rugged country. But that wasn't true for horses. Historian Mumey pretty much sums it up: "It was difficult to know who was in league with outlaws [back then], for many times men who appeared to be honest and trustworthy, were actually [or had been] associated with the thieves."[6]

Settlement, the telephone, fences, and improved transportation, decisively put the outlaws of old out of business. And Jackson's newspaper even took umbrage with the Hole's outlaw reputation, proclaiming: "Those who had settled there since the first homesteads in 1884 were solid citizens of the first order."[7]

Original settler Thomas E. Crawford, disgusted with the changes, remarked in his *Recollections*: "I made my last trip into

Jackson Hole during 1900... [it] was filled up with pilgrims and it didn't look good to me anymore." The Hole had become too civilized for all but rumored or retired horse thieves, scoundrels and desperadoes.

Regardless of the questionable beginnings of ranching in the Hole, by the start of the twentieth century it was fully legitimate. Holland applied for water rights in 1883 and Miller from Cache Creek in 1884, they were the first to do so in Jackson Hole,[8] indicating they eventually planned something more permanent than being outlaws. Not many years afterward Miller was running one of the largest herds of livestock in Jackson Hole.[9]

Miller married Grace Green in 1893 and they built the large log house (some call it Jackson's first trophy home) on what is today the National Elk Refuge. Miller's log home is still standing and is listed on the National Register of Historic Places, Holland married Maude Carpenter—who had a homestead to the north of his—in the late 1890s; and John Carnes's wife, Millie Sorelle, was a Bannock Indian.

In those years, Holland was regularly making snowshoe and horseback trips across the Pass to Victor—not to conduct outlaw activities, but for the benign purpose of delivering mail for the community and to check on his property and investments in Teton Basin. Authors Bonney and Bonney refer to Cal as a "crony" of John Holland's, and an inductee into the brotherhood. However, the knowledge gap for Cal's whereabouts and activities from the time of his arrival in Jackson Hole in 1898 until around 1912, which had made it easy to claim he was engaged in outlaw activities, now no longer exists.

John Holland and John Carnes sold their Nowlin Creek homesteads to David and Ben Goe in 1900, and skedaddled from the Hole around that time. Carnes moved on to Fort Hall, Idaho.[12] John Holland drifted across the Pass to his Teton Basin ranch at Horseshoe Creek, closer to where his wife's family resided.

At age forty-six, Holland served as a witness for Cal's Bates homestead application in 1901, listing his place of residence as Fremont County, Idaho and occupation as rancher.[13] Obviously, he and Cal were neighbors and stayed in touch. Sometime later Holland moved on to Salem, Oregon, where he opened a hotel. Cal said, "[I] took down a [railroad] carload of horses and cattle for him."[14] Holland died at age sixty-five from infection resulting from an accidental glass cut, but not before suffering two different amputations on the gangrenous leg.[15]

Carnes, a twice wounded Civil War veteran and Indian fighter, died in 1931, at age eighty-five, on the Hutchison Ranch at Fort Hall, Idaho, after his sight failed. His obituary says, "...at one time he was deputy sheriff and was sent to disperse a band of horse and cattle thieves that infested the [Jackson Hole] region." This is undoubtedly reference to the Cunningham Cabin incident. Carnes was quoted: "We were sent in there after them and they are there yet."[16]

Virtually all settlers in the Hole prior to and around 1900 started cattle ranches. While the ranches were generally small, cumulatively they amounted to a large number of cattle and horses. When once asked if there were any cattle in the Hole when he arrived there, Cal replied: "No great amount..." but then went on to recall settlers who ran cattle: "Cunnigham, Giltner, Leek, Redman, Miller..."[10] He could have named virtually every settler in the Hole.

By 1906, 4,072 cattle and horses were being permitted on the adjacent Forest Reserve alone.[11] Boiling it down, the Hole's ranches offered work for a skilled bronc buster, cowboy and horsemen like Cal. And we can figure Cal did ranch work and odd jobs for Turpin, Holland, Miller and other settlers at times, besides working for the Park and Forest Service.

There has been considerable myth and mystique associated with Flat Creek Canyon and a cabin that once existed there. It figures largely into stories about Cal's supposed rustling activities. In Cal's own words: "[In my early years in Jackson] I sometimes lived [in the cabin] up in the [Flat Creek] canyon where the horse thieves took the horses." In later years he'd embellish it: "All I had to do was to put up two pair of boards and that shut the whole canyon off...from there I could see the sheriff a comin' and a gonin'."[17]

However, his first statement implies the horse thieves were using the canyon before he lived there. A footnote by historians Bonney and Bonney states: "Cal told Charlie Peterson it was Holland who originally built the canyon corrals."[18]

Who originally built the cabin Cal and others used in Flat Creek Canyon is not certain, but it wasn't Cal, and he certainly did not live there in winter in those years. The old dirt-roofed cabin would have only been used seasonally.

Jackson old-timer Charlie Peterson referred to the structure as "the old trapper's cabin."[19] In an earlier, 1972 transcribed interview, Peterson mentioned a cabin used by trapper Billy Biers, located up in Flat Creek. According to author Jay Lawson, trappers Billy Bier (also spelled Bierer) and Albert Nelson built the cabin on Flat Creek in the fall of 1894.[20] Biers was considered to be Jackson Hole's last mountain man. Others, such as turn of the century sheriff and game warden Josiah "Si" Ferrin, as well as rancher Frank Peterson, also used the cabin.

This brings us back around to Eastern journalists who bought into Cal's stories, to wit: "Cal blandly explained that he merely helped himself to horses...[and] Flat Creek Canyon was ideal for hiding his stolen horses."[21] Cal's alleged use of Flat Creek Canyon for hiding stolen horses simply doesn't match the evidence, but it is consistent with his propensity for spinning yarns.

Perhaps closer to the truth concerning Cal's rustling activities, Felicia Gizycka remembered Cal earnestly telling her: "...he [had] wintered along the southern route, camping in the desert, and Quincy, one of Cal's pack mares, had come along at the end of a rope one dark night in Quincy, California." This would have been stealing, but it was not an uncommon open range practice when traveling through an area; it was euphemistically called "picking up extras." While it tended to irritate the livestock's real owner, it was not on the same level as organized rustling. Significantly, Felicia added, "Quincy was the last horse he ever stole."[22] Maybe the only one, too?

In his later years, Cal was asked, "What breed of horse was your favorite?" He replied, "Kentucky-Morgan." Then he went on to explain the parentage of a local line of horses came from five thoroughbred horses—four two year old fillies and a valuable stud—Ed Harrington had allegedly stolen while working at the Denver racetrack stables (not rustled from open range on the prairies) and eventually brought into Jackson Hole, after first hiding them over winter on the Fort Hall Indian Reservation supposedly with John Carnes' help.

Frank Peterson at the "trappers cabin" in Flat Creek.
Courtesy of JHHSM, 1993.4807.015.

They bred the fillies with the stallion then shot the stud and raised the colts. "They couldn't keep him, y' know. Someone would come along and notice him right away," Cal said.

He, of course, claimed no part in stealing the horses, but according to his statements he did acquire their offspring for breeding purposes as did others, no doubt, in Jackson Hole.[23]

Cal's Teton Valley neighbors didn't believe his "self-professed horse thief" stories. Lifelong Teton Valley resident Grant Thompson, whose father was born in 1919 in Cal's cabin at Bates (which their family had leased), scoffed at the idea, saying, "He [Cal] wasn't a horse thief."[24]

Long-time Teton Valley rancher Oren Furniss, whose family's homestead adjoined Cal's, after a thoughtful pause simply allowed, "It was hard to make a living in those days,"[25] implying people sometimes turned their heads away from what may have been done out of frontier necessity.

But again, during that time period, Cal was juggling the work demanded by his Desert Entry homestead across Teton Pass at Bates, and apparently simultaneously doing seasonal ranch work in Jackson, as well as working for the Park and Forest Service, too. He was rustling up a living, so to speak, as best he could. Since winter pretty much closed off the way in and out of the Hole in those days, it wouldn't have left him a lot time for organized horse rustling.

The telephone made its debut in the Hole in 1905. The Forest Service greatly expanded the lines in 1907,[26] and the influx of honest citizenry into Teton Valley and Jackson Hole, and improved communications through the telegraph and telephone, simply weren't conducive to outlaw activities. And by the twentieth century, ranchers and townspeople simply wouldn't have put up with their livestock going missing or having outlaws operating right under their noses, even though many enjoyed perpetuating the outlaw myths.

Nevertheless, it's true that Flat Creek Canyon may have been used at one time or another in the 1880s and early 1890s to hide horses whose true ownership was questionable—as possibly were Flat Creek meadows, Leek's Canyon, and the top of Miller's Butte. That Cal himself was actually involved in horse rustling in the Hole and that he used Flat Creek canyon for hiding stolen horses now appears very doubtful. It's more likely he was joshing folks with stories he had picked up from oldtimers about events that had actually taken place some number of years before his arrival in Jackson Hole. Cal's Wild West tales however, were, as mentioned, eagerly picked up and passed along in Jackson Hole folklore by local historians, Cissy Patterson's biographers and Cissy herself.

It's easy to guess how rumors started and circulated back then. Imagine two oldtimers sitting around jawing when a scruffy cowpoke rides past them. One of the old men nudges the other and jokingly whispers, "Hey, there goes one of the gang of six." Later they recognize the same rider again and one of them guffs, "That there's the gang of six horse thief again." The cowboy overhears the horseplay and says, "Yup, they was all caught, 'cept me." Much to their common delight, they've invented an entertaining joke. It gets passed around, the rumor repeatedly replayed and improved upon. After all, what other entertainment was there? Should a wide-eyed dude take them seriously, all the more fun.

Undeniably, though, Cal lived a rugged and demanding life during his early years in the Hole and Teton Valley. A live-and-let-live philosophy, and being in with the brotherhood and tight-lipped, helped assure one's survival in those times, especially when the only law was "mountain law."[27]

But the fact remains that around the turn of the twentieth century most Jackson Holers had stopped sleeping with their horses to protect them from rustlers. Historian Doris Platts' summation in *John Cherry: His Lies, Life and Legend*, applies to much of the Hole's early citizenry and history of that era, and especially to the likes of Cal: "We chuckle at how he has [or they have] succeeded in playing with the truth and in confounding us."[28]

10
Outfitting and Guiding

After returning from the Forest Service in California in 1908, Cal became involved in outfitting and guiding hunters. Cal said, "Holland had some big hunters...Boston shoe man, Count de Turin from Italy, Lord Morton, Governor of India..."[1] It seems likely Carrington may have gotten into guiding by first wrangling for Holland and his clients.

According to his 1957 interview, some of the first "dudes" Cal guided after quitting the Forest Service was Struthers Burt's party, around 1908-09. It included Burt, his wife and sister, Louis Joy and his wife, Doc Kyle and his wife and niece, and others in the group. "That was Burt's first trip...I bought his first horse."[2] There's an early photograph that may have been taken on this trip showing

Carrington and Holland with a party of three others. The five men had been hunting antelope.

When Cal had been associated with anybody or anything he'd invariably put himself in a proprietary position in his telling about it. Some of his perspective on that first meeting with Struthers Burt, as told in a 1957 interview, was: "That was Burt's first trip, and that fall he wanted me to buy some horses [for] the next year. He wanted to take my [Bates] ranch and go in with me and I wouldn't do it. I dunno how we'd come out, he's ejicated and I ain't. I'm afraid he'd pencil me out. But we was together, I think, nine seasons..."[3]

Cal claimed to have had other exclusive clients, too—a rich Englishman named John: "We were out six weeks...got over in Hoback Basin. They brought very little drink. They'd take coffee or tea. Cook would make cake and they'd sit there for...hours, chattering and drinking tea."[4]

John, the Englishman, said to Cal, "Better catch a cow and have some fresh milk."

"So I roped one and squeezed out what I could and that impressed him. He wanted to take me to India with him."

In those years, the elk in Jackson Hole were being forced off their traditional winter ranges in the valley by settlement and many were dying. Cal recalled, "I didn't see any [elk calves] for three years. All the yearlings died. They was piled in Flat Creek Canyon. I lived up in the canyon then where the horse thieves took the horses...I seen little elks piled up there three-four high."[5]

Cal apparently spent enough time traveling across the Pass from Teton Valley to Jackson and back that the wagon freighters knew him. There was one particular bad stretch of wagon road called the "red mud hole," located on the top of the

Cal Carrington in angora chaps with horse, c 1915.
From Jackson Hole Journal *by N. Burt;*
courtesy of University of Oklahoma Press.

Pass. An anonymous freighter told a story that one day he saw a hat floating in the mud hole. Lifting it up, he found Cal Carrington underneath.

"By golly, Cal, you sure have got into it," the freighter exclaimed, "I'll go down to Victor and get you some help."

"Never mind," Cal replied, "I'm a'horseback and think I'll make it."[6]

In traveling back and forth from Jackson Hole, Cal would stop over with his old friend, Jim Berger. Cal no doubt looked forward to those visits, since he probably was tired of cooking his own elk meat. Jim's life took a different turn when he settled down to farming and married Edith Odessa Parsons. Jim sold his original homestead near Bates and moved his family to Victor. They lived at the main turn in the road at the south end of Teton Valley (on the west side), where the road led north to Driggs.[7] Jim and Dessa had four children, the oldest, a son, was born in 1907. Berger died in 1963 and is buried in the Victor cemetery.

Somewhere around this time, Cal and his neighbors had a disagreement with a sheepman grazing in Twin Creek near his Bates ranch. "On Twin Creek they was bedding their sheep right alongside the creek, families below was using the water. Allen, Berger, and Briggs come down to the cabin and got me. We went out there and asked if he'd take his sheep off the creek. Well, the young fellow, he claimed he'd as much right there as anybody, and he talked back. I hadn't said anything. Finally, I told him, 'We didn't come up here to discuss laws or anything else. We asked you to move the sheep off the creek and bed 'em back further.' An instead of answering me, he turned up his nose at me. And I smacked him one right now. Wal, he moved the sheep and there was no more trouble there."[8]

Teton Valley, although settled predominately by Latter-day Saints, wasn't without its rowdy side, too: "Thar were some good times at Victor," Cal once recalled, relishing the memory, "...dances at the Old Shanty. I'd go there a'horseback from the ranch at Bates, then we'd go to John's still to get a bottle. I wouldn't get back to the ranch 'til sun up."[9]

Cal and his cohorts were engaging in the traditional frontier pastime of hell raising. As Maggie McBride noted in her journal, when one of her party's wagons broke down near Driggs on the Fourth of July, 1897, while on the way to Jackson Hole, "they were invited to a dance, but declined because most of them [the men inviting them] were drunk."[10]

Cal also said, "[In Jackson Hole] there are all kinds of parties, generally around Christmas and Fourth of July, never went home 'till the sun come out. Dance, tell yarns... At the time I hit Jackson there was Cora Nelson and two of the Davis girls wasn't married. Then the school mums comes in. We [the bachelors] had a helluva time pushing one another out of the way. They [the school marms] made up a song"—

> Jackson Hole, good ol' Jackson Hole;
> Nobody's in a hurry;
> It's a sin to worry...

"Pretty near all the oldtimers had some kind of music box, accordion, mouth organ, banjo or fiddle—made lots of noise."[11]

By the early 1900s, Teton Valley sported a number of dance halls—at Badger (Felt), Victor, Driggs, and elsewhere in the valley. It was said, "Victor's Log Cabin Inn served whiskey to anyone old enough to push a quarter over the bar."

Beesley's Dance Hall in Driggs hosted gifted local musicians, particularly fiddlers. Teton Valley's settlement was not all monotony and work without play, people showed up to these places and events in number by horseback, horse and sleigh, horse and buggy, and in later years, rag-top, wooden-spoke wheeled cars.[12]

Asked if anyone ever got rough at these dances, Cal responded: "Always waited 'till the dance was over. Had a sociable time...women folks wrapped kids in blankets and danced all night."[13]

Another amusement around that time was "prize fighting" (boxing). In his 1957 interview, Cal remembered "Bed Parker and Lum Nickerson was Teton Basin's prize fighters. They bet horses; didn't have no money. They went over to Jackson, an' Jake Jackson was the fighter there. Wal, it didn't last long, just a spat or two. They lost some horses. Jake was our champeen...They wasn't satisfied with that, so they got a fellow from Butte to come down and he was training over in the Basin. He was boxing everybody to get in shape. I had the gloves on with him; couldn't hold a hand to him. He'd tap me on the snoot any time he wanted to."

When winter set in, Cal generally crossed back over to Teton Valley. Sometimes he rode south out of the mountains into warmer climes, in Cal's words, "to winter along the southern route." After 1899, he could take the train from Rexburg.

In 1912 the Oregon Short-Line railroad, a subsidiary of the Union Pacific, was completed into Driggs. It was extended to Victor the next year. Victor became the end of the line. The railroad linked Teton Valley to the outside world, which locals colloquially called "out below." Importantly, the railroad provided a means for ranchers and farmers in the high mountain valleys surrounding the Tetons to market their livestock and produce.

But Jackson Holers still had to seasonally drive their livestock, and haul their produce by horse-drawn wagons across the demanding and hazardous 8,431-foot Teton Pass in order to reach the railhead. To accommodate all that, the Forest Service began grading the Pass road in 1912.

It was the practice of Jackson Hole ranchers back then to work together in the annual market roundup. Rancher Clifford Hansen recalls that in autumn they would all drive their steers into holding corrals located above Wilson, where they'd overnight. The next morning, beginning at dawn, they'd combine the stock into one herd of about 300-400 head and drive them across Teton Pass in one long day to the Victor railhead. Mostly, they met little or no traffic on the road. The drive was probably anticipated, so others would avoid travelling over the pass on that day if they could. The cattle were held in stockyards or pens provided by the railroad and fed a little hay and water until they could be loaded up. The Victor stockyards were intentionally located northwest of the depot to keep the rarified odors downwind. Generally, the cattle were shipped to Omaha. The cowboys and ranchers would spend a rowdy night at Victor's Killpack Hotel in sort of a seasonal celebration before heading back home over the pass. [14]

It speaks loudly of Cal's skills that he was hired as the first ranch foreman for the Bar BC homesteaded by Struthers Burt and Horace Carncross. They were impressed with Cal, as Burt would later attest: "He was a top cowhand...You didn't ask him to do ordinary chores around a ranch, such as fencing, ditching or haying. Those tasks were for a lower order of men known as ranch hands."

Cal was credited for instructing Burt in "the ways of ranching, livestock and the hills." [15] It was a considerable compliment because Burt was no tenderfoot, himself. Regarding Cal's rumored bad character, about which local gossips had warned him, Struthers Burt wrote: "I have never known in all my life a more honest man, or one more sensitive to obligation; he refuses to be under obligation to any one, and he is not happy until he has paid a favor back." [16]

11

Dude Wrangling

The short-line railroad into Victor opened the door for a mini-boom in tourism. Struthers Burt and his partner, Horace Carncross, turned their Bar BC cattle enterprise into a dude ranch. It was the second dude ranch to be established in Jackson Hole, and it became one of the most renowned.

In 1912, Burt and Carncross struggled to complete cabins and a main house for their first guests. In 1917, they expanded the guest ranch. Charlie Fox, a local contractor, and crew were "hired to do some buildin'."[1] Many of the old ranch cabins and buildings are still standing today within what is now Grand Teton National Park. Cal recalled, "Burt had a lot of problems before him. The building of that layout, and the carpenters, and a lot of those people under him...a lot of disagreeable things come up. The boys what he got was none too good, I told him that."[2]

Burt made Cal "head guide in charge of pack outfits," claiming, "there wasn't a horse Cal couldn't gentle, and not a wild animal he couldn't outwit."[3] Cal allowed, "It was time to get respectable and go into dudin'."[4] Cal said, "[Burt] brought out a lot of dudes from the East...good ones. Most of them was millionaires—Porter, Hemingway, Beau Reece...Reece was Mrs. Ryerson's brother, he got drowned on the Titanic...several artists [and] Princeton students."[5]

John Cherry worked at the Bar BC in the beginning, too, as did many other early day Jackson figures. It was one of the few job opportunities that paid in hard currency. There's no doubt Cherry set the bar high for the ranch's wranglers in spinning Wild West tales for the dudes.

Whereas work clothes for Cal before this may have consisted of overalls, a blue denim shirt, neckerchief, and boots, employees of the Bar BC guest ranch were a more colorful lot. They wore corked mustaches, fancy boots decorated with steer head stitching, big spurs, chaps of leather or angora, great gold and silver belt buckles, tight custom-made riders, colorfully designed shirts, loose gay neckerchiefs, and always a big hat. Nathaniel Burt summed it up: "...they possessed an aura of glamour...associated with wranglers, guides, ropers, and horse breakers."[6]

One thing certain to make Cal lose his professional composure, though, was if one of the dudes, when they headed out with a pack string, asked, "Where are we going to spend the night?"

Cal would pretend not to hear. If the dude persisted, Cal would raise both fists to heaven in silent supplication, and then

The remains of the original 1912 Bar BC Ranch lodge building
in Grand Teton National Park.
Photo by the author.

turning on the unfortunate questioner he'd thunder: "Look at
them thar hills! How do I know where we're a-goin to camp? I ain't
been there for a year. Maybe there's no grass left. Maybe it ain't
there no more. How do I know?"[7]

Cal generally stayed at the Crabtree Hotel when attending
rodeos in Jackson. Nathaniel Burt, who did not hold Cal in as
high esteem as did his father, Struthers, was disgusted on one
occasion because he and Cal ended up sharing a room (and bed?)
together in "Number 8." Inside the hotel room they could plainly
hear booted footfalls, voices and rowdy laughter in the hallway, as
well as snoring through the "flimsy room partitions."[8] Cal always

spent lots of time back in the hotel kitchen, "sittin' around and chewin' the fat" with Rose and Henry Crabtree.[9]

Cal and other Bar BC cowboys undoubtedly participated in the rodeo events.[10] Nathaniel thought Cal was a "wild man," but conceded "he added spice to the Bar BC setup, especially for the dude girls."[11]

Picture how incredulous Cal's stories about dude wrangling must have appeared to his friend Jim when Cal would stop off at Berger's place on the way back to Bates after his work at the Bar BC was over for the season.

12
My God the Count!

In the summer of 1916 providence provided a dramatically lucky break for Cal, fortuitously transforming his life forever. A countess and heiress to the *Chicago Tribune* fortune, Eleanor "Cissy" Patterson Gizycka, and her eleven year old daughter, Felicia, arrived at the Victor, Idaho, railhead with seven trunks and a French maid, en route to vacation in Jackson Hole. [1]

Cissy was restless after separating from her husband Count Josef Gizycka, from the Polish sector of the Russian Empire. Her much publicized divorce trial didn't actually take place until a few years later in Chicago.

Cissy, Felicia and the maid had traveled cross country on the Union Pacific and then by the newly opened Oregon Short Line from Ogden. Air conditioning had not yet been invented. The

Early day Union Pacific Railroad advertisement.
Courtesy of American Heritage Center, University of Wyoming.

The railroad depot at Victor, c 1950.
Photo courtesy John Wasson.

prairie sun relentlessly beat down on the Pullman car. The heat and dust were nearly unbearable. When windows were opened for relief, smoke from the engine blew in, blackening them and the other passengers with a layer of soot.

On the final leg of their journey, between Ashton and Tetonia in Teton Valley, everyone excitedly rushed to the windows to peer into the canyon defile when they crossed the giant eight-hundred-foot span, 155-foot-high Bitch Creek trestle; the longest on any Short-Line branch.

That night they boarded at the Killpack Hotel, Victor's "largest and most luxurious hotel,"[2] where Felicia remembered "...a sign saying *Loby* was a gathering place for cowpokes who sat chewing tobacco and aiming in the general direction at a row of tall brass spittoons; ...the rooms were filthy and the beds unmade."[3]

Regardless, Nathaniel Burt claimed, "Victor was the van of progress,"[4] But if Victor warranted the title of "vanguard," it gives some indication of the rawness of the conditions in Teton Valley and Jackson Hole back then. For outsiders it appeared frightfully stark; literally, "the end of the line."

The Bar BC sent a team of horses and a crude ranch wagon to "drag them acrost" Teton Pass. Their arrival at the Bar BC that night, soaked from rain and covered with dirt, is Jackson Hole legend. Cissy raged when she found out there was "no electricity, hot bath, soft bed, nor dinner on a tray," imperiously announcing she was leaving the next day.[5]

In the morning, the prospect of the long, exhausting and dirty wagon ride back across Teton Pass, and the likelihood of an indefinite stay at the Killpack Hotel because of an infrequent train schedule, gave her pause; as no doubt also did the captivating view of the sky piercing Tetons. Instead, she sent the French maid and six trunks back and she and Felicia stayed the summer.

Cissy was led to vacation at the Bar BC by a wealthy Chicago friend, George Porter, who specifically advised her to collar Cal Carrington as her escort and guide.[6] But Cal, it turned out, was off purchasing "gentle squaw ponies" at an Indian Reservation for the Bar BC, most likely at Fort Washakie.[7]

His return trip would have involved driving the horses over one hundred miles, including crossing Togwotee Pass (meaning "spearthrower," named after a Shoshone Indian who guided government expeditions), a craggy mountain road that had been improved by the U.S. Army in the early 1900s. The route was not unfamiliar to Cal, however. As he would later tell in a 1957 interview, he had once ridden bucking horses in Lander. In any case, Cissy's first look at Cal may have been a thrilling one, as he no doubt made his return with the herd of horses a dust-filled dramatic moment.

As was common among aristocracy, Cissy was an accomplished rider and hunter. She planned on hunting big game while at the Bar BC and had brought along a 6.5 Mannlicher.[8] Cissy occupied herself with target practice until Cal returned.

Arrangements had already been made for Cal to take another party out on a pack trip when he returned, but that changed. Years later, Felicia disclosed, "Cissy bribed him with a huge bunch of money, the likes of which he had never seen."[9]

Cal was forty one, Cissy thirty five. On that first hunting trip with Cissy, Cal outfitted and packed them into Soda Fork on the Buffalo Fork of the Snake River, within today's Teton Wilderness. They required a string of ten pack horses to tote not just the camp equipment, but also Cissy's baggage. Cal and Cissy would be gone

The Countess of Flat Creek Ranch, Eleanor "Cissy" Patterson. *Courtesy of JHHSM, 1958.3401.001.*

hunting all day, leaving a bored adolescent Felicia in camp with the painfully shy wrangler who, according to her, "said absolutely nothing all day."[10]

They were out twenty-two days, subsisting on a spike bull elk Cissy shot for camp meat. She fascinated Cal. When they became snowed in, she read Tolstoy aloud to the four of them in the tent. She was unlike any other woman Cal had known, independent and able to both ride and shoot. She bagged a trophy bull elk: "...them fellars [at Ben Sheffield's near Moran] kidded me about my fancy dude," Cal said, "all right, she done it. Look...and I showed 'em the [bull elk's] head."[11]

Cissy was impressed with Cal's "tough self-reliance." Their pairing became one of the most glamorous and jawed about "dude-cowboy affairs" that Jackson Hole and perhaps the West has ever known. Gossip galloped up and down the Hole. Folks would say, "There goes Cal and the Countess."

Cal possessively referred to the Countess as "my dude." Cissy would refer to Cal for the rest of her life as "dear old Cal."[12] Nearly ten year later, in *Glass Houses*, Cissy portrayed a connection to her character "Ben" (who is readily recognizable as Cal) as one that was enduring for all time. "No—never goodbye between us. It wouldn't make any difference if we didn't meet [again] for a hundred years."

As recently as 2000-2001, the town of Jackson recalled their romance in *Petticoat Rules*, a musical comedy that played at the former Pink Garter Theater.

At a dance in Jackson, where "Cal monopolized Cissy," and that Felicia described as "cowboys hopping around like grasshoppers on the rough dance floor," someone was heard to remark, "the Countess was a great lady, but my God, *the count!*"[13] "My God, the Count!" was a phrase Cal was never allowed to forget, it became part of Jackson folklore. Cowboys enjoy horseplay and greeting Cal with, "My God, the Count!" ranked high among their boisterous jokes.

Not surprisingly, there was an ornery, self-protective side to Cal. As Nathaniel Burt recorded: "Cal would openly mock Cissy's suitors, mount them on dangerous horses, spit contemptuously when they tried to shoot, and make slighting references to their virility."[14]

Cissy adored Jackson Hole. It was a place she could be herself. She loved its natural beauty and called it, "a small secret valley which lay like a warm opal set in stone." It was also a place, as her daughter Felicia penned, "full of [colorful] characters who could be themselves without benefit of psychiatry or interference from the law."[15] People in Jackson Hole back then had the courage and freedom to live their lives as they wished and they displayed a tolerance for the differences in others. In those days the Hole was occupied by a classless society.

The next summer, 1917, Cissy returned and rented the entire White Grass Ranch. Cal, hat in hand, regretfully apprised Struthers Burt that he had decided it was his duty to become her foreman and take care of her, explaining: "She don't know nothing...She's a mighty nice woman and someone might get the better of her."[16] Moreover, the job must have paid more than Cal could ever have imagined in his wildest cowboy dreams. Nathaniel Burt later recalled his father, Struthers, was not too pleased at the time.[17]

13

A Tale of Two Ranches

In the summer of 1917, Cal took Cissy on a horseback ride to the outlaw's hideaway in Flat Creek Canyon beneath Sheep Mountain, the place where he had sometimes stayed in the early years when he first came into Jackson Hole. According to her biographers, "Cissy thought it was the most perfect spot she had ever seen." We cannot know whether Cal actually represented the canyon as his, but at that time he did not own it. It was National Forest land.

Histories generally state that Cissy wanted to buy it from Cal, and much to do is made about Cal's "reluctance" to sell. By some accounts, George Ross, a former employee of the Bar BC who became a part-time employee and a big-game guide for Cissy, was finally sent to Cal's homestead in Bates to fetch the deed from his trunk.[1]

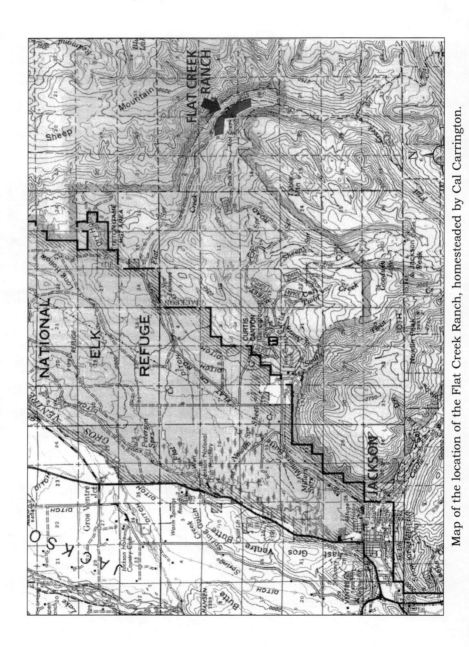

Map of the location of the Flat Creek Ranch, homesteaded by Cal Carrington.

Ross's errand, however, needs to be set in chronological context. It didn't happen until about six years after Cissy first saw the canyon. Of course Cal seemed "hesitant, unsure, and smilingly reluctant" about selling at first—he didn't have title. The stories of Cal's hesitancy to sell have been played up in the literature—"Cal was reluctant, highly reluctant..."[2] It was pure smoke and mirrors, a myth created by Cal and Cissy themselves and later perpetuated by journalists.

But there's no doubt Cissy was intrigued with Flat Creek Canyon and that spurred Cal. He wanted to please her. And it's safe to say Cissy was used to getting what she wanted. Together they schemed a way.

Having worked for the Forest Service, Cal was knowledgeable about the 1906 law allowing homesteading on the National Forest, and he knew how to go about it. Unlike the Desert Entry process at Bates, which had controlled his life for years, this time he was in charge. And, too, Cissy had the political contacts to intimidate and induce cooperation from agency administrators.

Cal proceeded to establish squatter's rights within the remote and rugged, steep-walled canyon, a scenic spot, but not a place where homesteading a farm or ranch normally comes to mind. Besides, the 1906 Act was intended to apply only to *tillable lands* within the National Forest system. Flat Creek Canyon most certainly did not qualify as tillable.

From 1918 through 1919, influenza struck Jackson Hole and its residents were occupied in fighting the devastating sickness. Neighbors took turns feeding each other's livestock in order to help out with the sick. There were only three automobiles in Jackson Hole back then, and the owners wore their tires out driving back and forth on the rough wagon roads providing assistance to those stricken by the flu.

It was that same year, in 1918, that Cal began cleaning up and improving the trapper's siwash cabin in Flat Creek, making it more livable, and he added or improved an outbuilding and corral. He also had the proposed property boundaries surveyed. By spring of 1920, "he had taken up residence and was clearing trees."[3]

According to the Flat Creek Ranch's website, "two years later he was running twenty-five cattle and horses." This would have been by permit on the National Forest. The livestock bore Carrington's brand—C A L. Neither the Flat Creek Ranch, nor Cissy, ever registered a brand.[4] In Dwight Stone's 1958 interview, Cal claimed he ran "...fifty head of cattle on the Forest Reserve," conceding, "It didn't work out too well."[5]

One has to wonder where the livestock were kept in winter. Livestock drifting down the canyon off the property or from the National Forest would have ended up on other homesteads or on the National Elk Refuge, which had been established in 1912. Locals referred to the Refuge as "the government's ranch."

Hauling enough hay into the isolated snowbound Flat Creek Ranch, or cutting sufficient quantities from the ranch's streamside sedge meadows, or "beaver meadows" as they were called, to overwinter the cattle and horses would have been an impossible task. Most likely, the ranch—that is, Cissy—paid for leasing overwintering ground, purchasing hay, and feeding the livestock on one of the Flat Creek homesteads, such as, perhaps, Frank Peterson's on Poverty Flats. In winter months, Cal had other fish to fry.

In those years, the road to Kelly wasn't where it is today. Rather, it took the route of the present day Elk Refuge road going east of the Gros Ventre Hills through Long Hollow, passing through homesteads en route. It was Cal's habit to stop off at the different homestead ranches and visit on the long ride to and from town.

Jackson resident Johnny Ryan, whose grandfather was Ben Goe, an early day settler and owner of the Cowboy Bar, recalls his "mother was always talking about Cal Carrington." When Cal would stop off at their Flat Creek homestead, "My mother," Johnny said, "would tell me to 'stay out of the way and don't say nothin'." John remembered, "He always liked to see Cal's horses, because he had good ones." Cal once warned him, "Kid, don't git behind that horse." Johnny said, "Everyone liked Cal."[6]

Historian Wendell Gillette's wife, Bertha, knew Carrington, too. Bertha's family also had a homestead located within today's National Elk Refuge. She described Cal as "a jolly, lanky, young man, as rigid and sound as a stake of iron...and never known to be without a broad smile."[7] Wendell and Bertha later moved to Victor, Idaho, but Bertha may have played a role in influencing her husband, Wendell, to research and chronicle his account of Carrington.

Frank Peterson's homestead was located on Flat Creek, at the western edge of Poverty Flats, also within today's Elk Refuge. Charlie Peterson Sr., Frank's son, remembers, "Cal a ridin' in with the north wind 'n' snow a blowin', wearing a heavy mackinaw coat. All the buttons was gone from it, and he had a piece of rope— string off a bundle of grain—tied round him to keep it closed."[8]

The Petersons kept a little band of elk in an enclosure. Like everyone else in Jackson in those days, they relied on game meat for subsistence. Frank was one of the Hole's original oldtimers. He had ridden with the 1893 Cunningham Cabin citizen posse and had also made the 1898 ascent of the Grand Teton with Billy Owen. He and Cal were longtime friends, and at times Cal would overnight with the Petersons in the comfort of their seven room log home before going on to town. The two men would sit next to a glowing woodstove swapping yarns and reminiscing about early day Jackson Hole.

On his lengthy horseback rides into town, Cal had time to amuse himself by inventing mischief, so when he was asked, "What are you a doin' up thar at the Countess' place?" he came back with: "I'm a beautifyin' it, makin' it real purdy."

Someone would get curious and take the bait, "How ya doin' that?"

"Well, I'm a buildin' bird houses an' putting them up on posts," Cal would reply with a grin.

Indeed, Bertha Gillette, for one, passed it around. "Cal was beautifying the ranch for the Countess by making and putting birdhouses up on poles, corners of cabins, and on fence posts."[9] It might have been true, but on the other hand, things must have been awfully slow at the ranch if Cal was building birdhouses.

Christmas rolled around and Cal faced the dilemna of what to get Cissy—a person who already had everything. On his rides to and from the ranch he had time to reflect on it. With a hint of devilment he composed and sent a letter to Cissy saying he had given her a cow for Christmas. He would care for it, but it was now *her* cow. Included with his letter was a bill of sale: "For value received I give to Countice Gizcka one spotted cow four years old branded CAL on left ribes." It was signed C.E. Carrington and witness by Gus Graceclose, the 25th day of December 1922.[10]

In those days, two odors permeated the town of Jackson—the livery stables and the aroma of hops from brewing beer. No one found either smell offensive. And hitching rails conveniently lined the streets in front of businesses.

During those years, Cal leased out his Bates ranch. From 1918-21, the Thompson family had the lease. Victor resident Grant Thompson's father, Charles Jr., was born there in 1919. Grant remembers a family story of how during those years, "they weren't able to pay the rent, their crops froze out." Cal didn't receive his rent money and rode over from Jackson. As he approached the cabin he began angrily shouting: "Charlie, get your wife, kids, horse and ass out of here."[11]

Cal attempted to physically throw Charlie off the place. "They wrestled around in the yard," as Grant's family story goes. "Suddenly Cal stopped, exclaiming, 'Dammit, I can't whip you, Charlie, I guess you're a stayin'." Mounting his horse, Cal rode away cussing and muttering he'd be back for his rent. The Thompson family came up with the rent money the next season.[12]

14
Among High Society

When Jackson Hole's interminable winter set in, Cissy would scoot back East to her family estates in Chicago, New York or Washington, at which time Cal would slip back into his old solitary ways. Sometimes, though, he would board the train at Driggs, travel the short line to Ogden, and from there ride the Union-Pacific back East or sometimes to California to join her.

As one writer described, "Cal was paraded around Chicago, Long Island and Washington in all his frontier flavor,"[1] with Cissy showing him off to her high-society friends. The Patterson Mansion at 11 Dupont Circle, acclaimed as the scene of many lavish parties[2] in Washington, D.C., became a familiar place to Cal. But as one might guess, not all of Cissy's family were impressed. One family member remarked, "Where did you dig him up?"[2]

Cal had learned from guiding wealthy clients at the Bar BC, that they put their pants on the same way he did. Well-heeled people with their luxurious and lavish lifestyles didn't intimidate him. However, his cowboy origins and ways fascinated them. If anything, he may have felt—but wisely did not openly display—contempt for the social mores of the hifalutin dudes. Instead, he demonstrated intelligent open-mindedness and was a quick study, adept at learning and adapting to whatever was socially expected or required. Cal appears to have epitomized a cowboy version of the Hollywood 1980s character *Crocodile Dundee*.

One thing troubling to Cissy though, who was touted as "brilliant, well read, and sophisticated," was that Cal didn't particularly like to take baths. He'd say, "baths weakened the constitution...hot baths robbed you of your manhood." Likewise, Felicia wrote, "Cissy could never get used to his wearing clothes that smelled and needed washing...she was forever telling him to 'go wash.'"[3] Cal likely had a Westerner's ambivalence towards water, in his mind it could end drought, but it also caused mud and flooding.

On the other hand, in the Old West, the cold climate and scarcity of hot water did not encourage frequent bathing. And as Cissy herself describes in *Glass Houses*, the smell of leather and harnesses, lathered horses, livery stables and "healthy, strong, unwashed men" was a heady and exciting part of her Western experience.

In 1922, Cal traveled abroad with Cissy and Nellie Patterson, Cissy's mother. They visited Paris, Berlin and Russian Poland. In Paris, Cissy took Cal to see the Eiffel Tower, cancan girls, and Josephine Baker, the famous black entertainer, who performed in the nude. They sat at Parisian outdoor cafes—Cal in his cowboy hat and best boots and Cissy glowing. Biographer Martin penned:

"Even the blasé Parisians must have stared as the cowboy and his red-haired lady rode horseback in the Bois de Boulogne."[4]

Cissy wrote to Jackson hotel proprietress, Rose Crabtree, with whom she had become good friends, saying "...she and Cal visited Napoleon's tomb and both of them cried from the majesty and beauty of the thing."[5] Rose raised an eyebrow at the idea of Cal Carrington weeping at a tomb.

Cal wanted to see Italy, Nellie Patterson didn't, so Cal went alone. In spite of it all, Cal never stopped being his own man. When he wanted to be with Cissy, he was, when he wanted to go elsewhere, he did. When he took a long time to return from Rome, Cissy wrote Rose: "I really have begun to fear something terrible has happened, although I'm sure the old simp is [merely] having the time of his life and is too busy to write. Or else he's in jail."[6]

The original restored Flat Creek Ranch lodge as it appeared in 2004.
Photo by the author.

15

Flat Creek Politics

In March 1922, after their return from Europe, about four years after he took up squatter's rights and made some "improvements," Cal applied for patent on the 149-acre Flat Creek Canyon tract.

Wearing his Western boots and cowboy hat, and emboldened with a letter of introduction to one of Cissy's social acquaintances, the powerful Senator Francis E. Warren of Wyoming, Cal strode into the Washington headquarters of the Forest Service. There he swore out a claim, stating: "He had occupied the Flat Creek homestead tract under squatter's rights since 1901."[1] That date was a stretch of the truth that would have made John Cherry proud. That may have been the year Cal first rode into Flat Creek Canyon or maybe first stayed overnight at the old trapper's cabin, but he could not have "occupied" it from that time in the manner stipulated by the 1906 Forest Homestead law. He obviously had been much too occupied elsewhere.

The Forest Homestead Act of 1906 was intended to apply only to "pre-determined tillable lands" within the National Forest system, and in order to "prove up," a claimant had to live on the land, build a home on it, make improvements, and farm it for at least three years.[2]

The politically overwhelmed local forest ranger who was asked to comment on the application fumbled for reply: "I'm not against the homestead, even though Cal's cultivation has consisted almost entirely of harvesting wild hay[3] [from the streamside sedge meadows]."

The ranger's statement ignored the 1906 law's requirements and could have been interpreted either way—for or against the application. It was dutifully filed away. But Flat Creek Canyon was never among the National Forest lands bona fide as tillable under the act by the Secretary of Agriculture, and cutting "wild hay" for horse feed wasn't farming, nor did the trapper's cabin technically qualify as a home built by the claimant.

In Cal's and Cissy's time, the valley above the ranch looked different than today. Rather than a lake, a stream cut through it, with beaver dams, willows and sedge meadows bordering it. Cal's description of it was that "there was a meadow up there half a mile long, not quite a quarter mile wide..." The "beaver meadows" were used for summer horse pasture and for "wild hay," however, none of it remotely qualified as "tillable agricultural land." These were the meadows (holding pasture) where rustled stock may have been kept before Cal's time. The present-day lake was created in the 1950s when, at that time, ranch caretaker Al Remington dammed the creek and flooded the sedge meadows to create a fishery.

Sometime shortly afterward, in 1922, in a whirlwind of travel for those times, Cal had managed to meet up with Cissy in Santa Barbara, California. Cissy was put off by the particular gathering of people she found herself with and tried to warn Cal away, but he showed up anyway. Cissy condescendingly remarked in one of her letters to Rose: "[Cal] will probably get mad and run off before we get tired of him..."[4] Cal was obviously a very busy man between operating two ranches and becoming an accomplished gadabout.

The initial homestead patent issued for the Flat Creek Ranch, No. 49044, was dated April 12, 1922,[5] but it got hung up in the bureaucracy. The Forest Service was not keen on opening the National Forests to homestead entry in the first place, and that application was not only legally questionable, but it went against the agency's internal policies.

Cissy, however, was used to getting her way. To put an end to further delay she enlisted the help of her friend, Senator Warren, who personally fired off a letter on November 15, 1922, to the Department of Interior's GLO flat out telling them to "expedite the matter [of the Flat Creek approval]." After that, the patent was approved in what must have been record time—two days later on November 17—and a follow up letter was promptly sent to the senator by the GLO informing him of the approval.[6]

Cal couldn't contain his ear-to-ear grin when he received and opened the official looking envelope at the Driggs post office. Inside was the patent document (H.E. 07481) for the Flat Creek homestead, approved by President Warren G. Harding on December 4, 1922.[7]

Rather quickly thereafter, in February 1923, Cal apparently overcame any of his previously much touted "reluctance" or "misgivings" and sold the property to Cissy for five thousand dollars.[8] As the story goes: "Cissy handed Cal a check saying, 'This is for the ranch, now you take it and shut up'." So while Cal did "shut up and take the money," it was under different conditions than legend has led us to believe. It would have been then that George Ross was sent to Bates to retrieve the homestead patent from Cal's trunk in the cabin where he was keeping it.

Cal didn't record his original homestead deed at the time of its receipt, but the property sale to Eleanor Gizycka was recorded in Jackson on February 28, 1923. Later, a warranty deed was also recorded by Cissy on March 10, 1924. Curiously, the 1924 warranty deed was prepared in San Diego, California. Additional evidence that Cal was not in Jackson that winter is that Cissy asked Rose Crabtree to keep an eye on the Flat Creek Ranch for her. Apparently, Cal or Cissy, or both together, spent the winter in San Diego that year.

During Carrington's years working to prove up on the Flat Creek Canyon property, while also pulling a salary from Cissy, it appears that few, if anyone, ever thought to ask, knew about, nor apparently even cared about his Desert Entry farm in Teton Valley. It's possible Cissy didn't know about his Bates property at that time either. Neither Felicia, in her writings, nor Cissy in her letters to Rose, makes mention of it until sometime after the Flat Creek homestead was patented. There is also no mention that Cal ever took Cissy to his Bates farm in all their time together.

Cal, obviously, was guilefully tight-lipped when it counted. He had spent much of his life spoofing greenhorns, dudes and bureaucrats and he must have smiled all the way to the bank after pulling off the Flat Creek caper. Most people still incorrectly believe or have the impression that Cal already owned the Flat

Creek Ranch when he first met Cissy. Even Felicia, who wrote: "...he had homesteaded the Flat Creek Ranch to hide his stolen horses;"[9] and Wendell Gillette who said "Cal built a small cabin in Flat Creek Canyon in 1898 and took up squatters rights, this he held secretly..."[10] Horse thievery indeed.

Cal was made foreman of Cissy's Flat Creek Ranch. It took several years to construct, because of the difficulty of transporting materials to the site. Author Bertha Gillette described Cal in those years as "the Countess's hired man, her horseman, her fixer-upper and tearer down."[11]

The completed ranch structures consisted of a lodge, several cabins, corrals and Cissy's little red barn, styled after Midwestern barns. Compared to historic photographs, the restored ranch looks much the same today as it originally did. It has been well maintained but remains delightfully unchanged. Only the stream-bottom meadows above the ranch have been modified by the creation of the dam and lake.

One of the several carpenters Cissy employed was Henry Crabtree, Rose's husband. Biographer Martin portrayed Cissy as being incredulous at the fact Rose had only known one man in her life, her husband. Cissy made it a point to tease and encourage Rose to have an affair. So while Henry was working up at the ranch, Cissy would write notes to Rose, which she'd have Cal deliver since there was no phone at Flat Creek. Once in Jackson, Cal would stay over at the Crabtree Hotel—to catch Rose up on how things were going at the ranch, perhaps?

Cal and Cissy's relationship was stormy. Felicia wrote that "they would have fights at the ranch that probably loosened the mountains and caused the famous GrosVentre landslide." After a fight, Cal would saddle his horse and ride down the canyon. He'd be gone for long periods, only to return muttering cuss words while he deftly unsaddled his horse. [12]

It's certain Cal used those occasions to get away over Teton Pass and check on his Teton Valley property. Oren Furniss, a Teton Valley neighbor, recalls that on one occasion Cal returned to find someone had taken up residence in his cabin. Oren remembers the uproarious scene, punctuated with loud cursing and yelling: "Cal run the trespasser off with his quirt." [13]

16
Famous Hunting Couple

Struthers Burt penned that "as a hunter Cal was intuitive...putting himself into the mind of the animal."[1] Cissy, a serious hunter herself, became Cal's protegé. One guide acknowledged, "She would go anywhere an elk went." Another, said, "She could hit an elk at four hundred yards.", This was undoubtedly with her favorite rifle, a 6.5mm Mannlicher carbine. Cal gave her a pair of black angora chaps to keep her warm on their autumn pack trips into the mountains.[3]

Their hunting trips together in the West and Canada continued for a period of years. Later, in 1939, the *Saturday Evening Post* would report: "Visitors to [Cissy's] Dupont Circle home were struck by the sight of thirteen heads and pelts [of grizzly bear, moose, elk, deer, bighorn sheep and mountain goat] which hung on the wall overlooking the grand staircase."

In 1921, Cissy decided she was going to be the first woman ever to run the River of No Return. She organized a party of about a half-dozen people, including another woman who she does not name, except as "R.E.," and an experienced river guide. Cal (pen named "Ben" in her story about the trip) went along as her "first mate." Cissy calls him her "philosopher, guide and friend." The river guide provided "a squared off at both ends...thirty feet long by eight drift boat...with two clumsy fore and aft sweeps for steering." Cissy categorized it as an "unlovely, but capable, little scow drawing only six inches of water."[4]

Cissy describes how, from Salmon to Riggins, Idaho, they ran the river's formidable white water rapids "shooting clear out of the water...sometimes lying flat to avoid the swinging sweeps"...in "grilling, frying heat"...and at night, "sleeping on sandbars;" and sometimes, with rattlesnakes showing up in camp.

She wrote in her journal, "The [Salmon River] country is wild, inaccessible and stupendous." Cal agreed, remarking, "The white man can never kill [all] the game off here." At Riggins they sold the boat, as there was no way to get it back to Salmon.[5]

One has to wonder how at ease Cal really was on the river. As a cowboy he had no experience in boating rivers, and once admitted, he never learned to swim because his horse could do it better.[6] Still, Cal was fascinated with the ranches along the Salmon River which remained mostly snow-free all winter, as compared to the rigors of ranching in Jackson Hole.[7]

Cal and Cissy also did some hunting and fishing along the way. At one point they spotted four mountain goats. One person in the party argued there were eight. Cal allowed how "every time a goat went behind a rock and came out again, [that person] counted it twice." In her boating story, Cissy also off-handedly mentions she and Cal had been hunting in the "savage, gloomy Wilson Canyon," on the Middle Fork of the Salmon, two years earlier. On that trip Cissy had taken two mountain goats.[8]

Sometime around 1923, Cal's friend, Frank Peterson, was supposed to have accompanied them as wrangler on a hunting trip into the west fork of Crystal Creek and to Granite Creek in the Gros Ventre Mountains. However, Frank had some critical ranch work that needed tending, so instead he sent his inexperienced teenage son, Charlie. Charlie recalls: "We wuz all gonna sleep under the stars, but then it began rainin'. I crawled under a tree, but Cal, he drug his saddle an' blankets into the tent with Cissy, an' stayed."[9]

Charlie divulged an embarrassment he suffered on that trip: "One night most of the horses got away from me. Cal saddled one of the others and set out after them. He finally caught up with the runaways nearly back at Flat Creek and brought them back to camp—all but one. Said he couldn't catch mine, so I had to walk for the rest of the pack trip. I never let those horses get away again."[10]

Charlie later became a hunting guide and outfitter himself, guiding renowned clients such as *Outdoor Life*'s gun editor, Jack O'Conner, on moose hunts in the Jackson Hole area.[11]

Under Cal's tutelage, Cissy graduated from deer, elk and bear to more elite and challenging big game—Rocky Mountain bighorn sheep. They pursued them out of Flat Creek Ranch on the windblown precipices of Sheep Mountain (Sleeping Indian), trailing their way up the steep, nearly impassable mountain with horses.

Cal helped Cissy pick out a pony that she named "Ranger." They declared he had been "born with nineteen legs" he was so surefooted. On the steep mountain slopes Cal would call back over his shoulder: "Loosen up on your [horse's] reins, he ain't a-goin' to fall, he's got four legs and twice as much sense as we have."[12]

Because of the rugged, high-elevation mountain terrain bighorn sheep inhabit, hunting them can be notoriously difficult. Cissy thrived on the challenge. In 1923 their obsession for sheep hunting took them to the Canadian Rockies in Alberta. Cissy also bagged a trophy bull moose in Canada. One source states: "They became known as the famous hunting couple from Jackson Hole."[13] Photographs of Cissy attest to their success at bagging trophy rams.

Cal was equally as good on foot in the mountains as he was on horseback. On one occasion, while hunting high among the crags, Cissy shot a full curl ram across a chasm. The animal tumbled into space and out of sight. She badly wanted the trophy-sized head, and implored Cal to retrieve it.

"How you gonna get it?" Cal asked, "I ain't noticed no airplanes around here."

Finally, Cal relented, climbing down over cliffs and talus rock and disappearing far below. Four hours later, he reappeared on a lower ledge, radiant and triumphant, carrying the magnificent head. Luckily, the horns weren't broken in the ram's fall.[14]

However, later, on that same trip, Cal and Cissy had a serious blow up that eclipsed all others. What caused the falling out may only be guessed. Cissy wrote Rose Crabtree saying Cal had been "a little treacherous and light fingered all his life...[and]

he has been both [with me]." She swore she would never trust him again. That winter she directed Rose Crabtree to have her horses taken care of, but specified "not in Cal's care."[15]

Cissy may have been fed-up, angry, spiteful, or maybe all of those, because the next summer, in 1924, she brought Elmer Schlesinger, a prominent Eastern attorney, with her to Flat Creek. Elmer had been courting Cissy for some time. His world, however, was New York City. To him, Jackson Hole was an alien place.[16]

Eleanor "Cissy" Patterson with her trophy bighorn sheep, c 1920s.
Courtesy of JHHSM, 1958.2183.001n.

17

Riffs and Rescues

In a seemingly awkward arrangement, Cal continued as the Flat Creek Ranch foreman. Cissy still relied heavily on him, but at times tension was so palpable you could have forked it like hay. Tempers flared, people were edgy. When Cal, having misplaced his knife, asked Cissy if she had seen it, she snapped, "It's in an employee where you stuck it."[1]

Both Cissy and Elmer always arrived in Jackson with enough cases of liquor to last their stay, especially during prohibition. According to accounts, Schlesinger was always very concerned about his whiskey bottles getting broken on the rough wagon ride into the ranch.[2]

Cissy was drinking more in those years, and she was a notoriously "mean drunk." Drinking brought out her violent temper. Cal, on the other hand, an employee informed, "got quiet when he drank. You wouldn't know he was drunk until he talked." Years before, Jackson settler Dick Turpin had accused Cal of "being Irish," saying, "Cal would drink anything."[3] Needless to say, the boozing contributed to some volatile and explosive altercations at the ranch.[4]

Cissy kept a Model-T Ford truck at the ranch. If Cal was annoyed or angry when he was driving, which he frequently was in those days, he would speed at twenty-five miles per hour, in a reckless fury, up or down the rough and narrow, winding wagon road with its precipitous drop-offs. Few today dare to travel the road at at that speed, even with modern 4-wheel drive vehicles. Somehow he—and those who may have had the misfortune to ride with him—survived.

On one occasion, teenaged Felicia—who Cissy described at that stage as being "about as easy to drive as a team of young bull moose"—forgot to close a gate, letting all the horses escape. It took Cal until nightfall to find them all and herd them back up the canyon. He notified Cissy when he got back, announcing, "A kid is an expensive proposition."

Later, Cissy fired Rex Ross, George Ross's son, after Cal complained a cow and calf Rex had let out of the corral had run off. But Rex denied it was his fault.[5] Rex was born at Teton, near where Teton Village is located today, and both he and his father also worked for the Bar BC Ranch.

Sometime around then, in a tantrum, Cissy tried to fire her maid, Aasta, but Felicia intervened. A knockdown dragout fight ensued between Cissy and Felicia with screaming, hair-pulling and clothes tearing. Felicia ended up riding away bareback on a pony that Cal had given her, using tied-together cotton socks for a halter. The incident caused quite a stir in Jackson. The town prattle about Felicia's bareback flight from Flat Creek became a Jackson Hole legend.[6]

In Jackson, Felicia went to the Crabtree Hotel and lied to Rose Crabtree: "Grandmother is sick and I have to go home." Not easily fooled, Rose asked, "How did you get the message–by Ouija board?"[7]

Felicia pulled her savings from the Jackson Bank, left her horse at the Jackson livery stable, took a stagecoach to Victor and caught the train to Salt Lake City, and then disappeared. By coincidence, in Salt Lake City she ran into Irvin Corse, who had just bought the Bar BC. Felicia confided to him she was running away to California.

A young reporter, Drew Pearson, who had been at the Flat Creek Ranch that summer, had a crush on Felicia. In California, after a few months of washing dishes and waitressing in a San Diego waterfront bar and men's club, staying in cheap boarding houses, and sharing an apartment with a Navy couple, Felicia began corresponding with Drew.[8]

After Cissy learned of Felicia's whereabouts through Irvin and Drew, she put Cal on a bus to San Diego to track her down and bring her home, not unlike what she might have had him do with her stray livestock.

It drew quizzical looks when the tall cowboy walked into the waterfront bar in San Diego wearing a big hat and high-heeled boots looking for Felicia, who was waiting tables. "Hey, Little Fellar, your mama sent me to look in on ya."

Once Cal determined Felicia was okay, he didn't try to persuade her to return. Secretly, he may have empathized,

Portrait of Felicia Gizycka as a young woman.
Courtesy of JHHSM, 1958.2468.001.

remembering when he, too, had run away. Moreover, he reckoned, at eighteen years of age, she was a grown woman.

Former director of Jackson Hole's museum, and an acquaintance of Felicia's, Robert Rudd, confirms Felicia was in San Diego around that time, and also that her good friend Dorothy Redmond Hubbard was attending school there. Bill Redmond, Dorothy's father, was an early homesteader in Jackson Hole who moved up to the Red Rock Ranch in the Gros Ventre in 1916, after selling his original homestead to Bert Charter, because he thought Jackson had become "overcrowded." Charter, it's believed, had once been a member of Cassidy's Wild Bunch, but had become respectable. According to Rudd, Cal spent time in San Diego at Cissy's bidding serving as a chaperone for the two girls.[9]

Cal very likely was already familiar with San Diego. It was a spot early Jackson Holers moved to for retirement. The first settler on the west bank of the river, Bill Menor, who built and operated Menor's Ferry at what is now Moose, started the trend by retiring there in 1918. By the 1930s, so many Jackson Holers had moved or retired there they were able to hold reunions.[10]

Understandably, Cal was not quick to turn around and head back to Wyoming. The perfection of California's climate enticed him to poke around some. Just north of San Diego, at Encinitas, near the ocean, he discovered a 23.72-acre triangular-shaped tract for sale. The balmy, live oak and citrus tree covered property contrasted sharply with Idaho and Wyoming's monochromatic winter landscape. Cal's attraction to the idyllic setting reveals an impressionable side—Encinitas claimed to be "the flower capital of the world."

Presumably, it was around this time, instinctively and without deliberation, Cal purchased the Encinitas tract. No doubt he paid cash for it. He was not short on greenbacks having worked for Cissy and after selling her the Flat Creek Ranch. Mortgages were not the way he did things. A number of years later he acquired another parcel—a lot—next to what is today's Moonlight Beach State Park. Typical of him, he apparently did not record the deeds. For years he told no one about his southern California properties, while over time their values soared like a raven in a thermal updraft crossing the Tetons.[11]

In 1924, Cissy wrote Rose, "It always worries me to think of him [Cal] living alone [in winter]. I suppose he hibernates like an old bear in his cabin."[12] Her worry was misplaced, "hibernating" was something Cal never considered.

Drew Pearson courted Felicia in San Diego and they married in 1925, but divorced in 1928. She lived what one chronicler termed "a life of international frivolity," and ended up marrying and divorcing two more times. Felicia pursed a career in writing. She and Cissy had one thing in common— they were both committed alcoholics—but through it all Felicia continued to write. And she never gave up her friendship with Cal. However, she never returned to Jackson again until she was fifty years old.[13]

Cal continued seasonally as Cissy's foreman. In 1925 Jackson newspapers reported a total of six hundred dudes vacationed in Jackson Hole. From a 1958 recorded interview, we know Cal guided his clients into the Tetons on pack trips. He knew and followed all the high mountain trails, amid the snowbanks and alpine flowered splendor up Phillips Canyon to Phillips Pass and on to the Teton Crest, past Housetop Mountain to Marion Lake, and north from there to wherever time allowed, finally looping back down the side canyons into Jackson Hole.

In his 1958 interview he said his "most favorite view of the Tetons was from Table Mountain," and he claimed to have frequently ridden up the trails to it on horseback.[14] There is a Table Mountain (Table Rock) on the west side of the Tetons, but there is also a Table Mountain in the Gros Ventre Mountains a few miles southwest of the Flat Creek Ranch. Both provide direct views of the Grand. Certainly, Cal had to be aware of this. Was he amusing himself by condescendingly toying with the interviewer and us? Locals generally call the mountain on the Teton Valley side Table Rock, so likely Cal was referring to Table Mountain in the Gros Ventre.

In the autumn, Cal would outfit and guide hunters for the ranch. Head mounts of big game taken by Cal from around this period hung in the Wort Hotel in Jackson[15] up until recent time. In 1926, he took four hunters from Philadelphia (many dudes originated from Pennsylvania in those years due to Struthers Burt's connections there and at Princeton) into the Soda Fork on the Buffalo River, and also set up another hunting camp for the ranch several miles away.

After dark one evening, Reed Henry, the guide from the other camp, showed up, obviously distraught, looking for Cal. One of his hunters, "a great big strapper [football player] from Princeton University," as Cal put it, "had gotten himself lost." Cal went looking for the man early next morning, cut his tracks and trailed him. "I found him sitting under a tree along Blackrock Creek." Word of the wilderness rescue got back to town, elevating Cal's reputation to local hero status.[16]

Pack string and riders crossing in front of the Tetons in Jackson Hole. *Harrison Crandall photo, courtesy of Quinta Pownall, JHHSM 1958.0967.001P.*

18

Africa Safari

For years, Cal had expressed an interest in hunting in Africa. Some say he had saved his money, others believe Cissy—the Schlesingers—arranged it as a reward for finding the ranch's lost hunter. No doubt both are true. In any case, in 1927, Cal's desire to hunt in Africa became a reality. [1]

In a letter to Rose Crabtree, Cissy stated Cal was among the one hundred thousand spectators who attended the Dempsey-Tunney fight at Soldier Field in Chicago. Then he traveled by rail to his East Coast port of departure and several days later boarded an East Indian freighter going to St. John's, New Brunswick, before crossing the Atlantic bound for Mozambique, British East Africa, by way of the Suez Canal. Cal had his own cabin and a black East Indian youth just to attend to his needs.[2] He wrote Cissy, "there was even a porthole to throw his washwater out." It appears to have been a voyage in the tradition of nineteenth-century adventurers!

Once in Africa, he traveled by train to Nairobi, and then on to Lake Albert where the railroad ended. There he bought a secondhand "tin-lizzie"—a Model T-Ford touring car. The factory price on the new Model-T in those days was $395.

Alone, Cal toured East Africa, inquiring the way to hunting country and subsisting on game he shot with his 9mm rifle, a gun Cissy had given him for the trip. He hunted hippos from boats at close range. Cal claimed the Natives called him *anakosea-aka!*, in Swahili—essentially "he never misses" or "never miss." Struthers Burt wrote, "At night he would close the car windows and go to sleep with lions prowling about."[3]

From there, historian Gillette recorded, he hired a guide and eight porters, and obtained safari supplies and equipment to travel three hundred miles cross-country hunting on foot. Sometimes he met up with other white hunters who joined him. He killed three or four elephants with the 9mm rifle. Once, while out with a "tusk hunter from the Barbary Coast," a bull elephant he had wounded charged him at close range, nearly trampling him. It had one hundred twenty pounds of ivory, which he sold for four dollars a pound, more than covering the one hundred dollar license fee. Cal commented, "Elephant [meat] is sweet, but awful coarse and tough."[4]

Cal returned home to Teton Valley around December 1927. Years later when asked what his best experience in Africa had been, he replied, "Well that's kinda hard, cause something [exciting] happened pretty near every day."[5]

Cal shipped his trophies back from Africa, and they eventually arrived and sat at the Victor railroad freight dock without notice. In a letter to a friend, Goldie Chisman, Cal wrote, if I had took the noon train [home] my trophies would of been left [sitting] in Victor for goodness [k]nows for how long."[6]

For the rest of his life, Cal would spin yarns about Africa. He did not simply just tell stories about his experiences, he'd put on a one-man show, entertaining by imitating animal sounds such as elephants trumpeting and even pantomiming giraffes mating.[7]

He was gone nearly a year on the African safari. Once back in Jackson, he resumed his job of ranch foreman for Cissy, seasonally wrangling dudes, guiding hunters and spending winters in Teton Valley, California and sometimes Mountain Home, Idaho.

After Africa, his old life may have seemed a bit tame. So maybe it shouldn't be too surprising that a few years later, the 1930 census somehow recorded Enoch Carrington at both Los Angeles, California and Cape Nome, Alaska.[8] We might surmise Cal had taken a junket to Nome to see the storied gold fields, not to work in the mines.

170 *I Always Did Like Horses & Women*

19

Tea Cups and Silk Socks

Cal had always tended to roam. This leaning was now fueled by his exposure to possibilities and aided by connections with well-to-do dude clients and friends. He became sort of a gadabout. As a colorful character, he had acquired instant insider status back East. Struthers Burt characterized Cal's excursions as "triumphal." In Chicago he became a "civic institution," falling in with the "Alley Bazaar crowd," meeting opera singers, actors, Follies girls, and millionaires.[1] Burt said "...when I went through Chicago...all I had to do to introduce myself was to mention Carrington's name. Cal was so popular in Chicago that, as he himself expressed, 'he had to make his getaway from that city between sundown and sunup'!"[2]

Cal Carrington and Felicia Gizycka and her daughter Ellen on the street in front of Cissy Patterson's mansion in Washington, D.C., c 1930. *Courtesy of Eugene Downer, publisher* Teton Magazine.

In Philadelphia, he went fox hunting with the city's elite equestrians. Never having ridden an English saddle before, he was unseated several times and unceremoniously dumped onto the ground, much to the amusement of his hosts and embarrassment to his cowboy pride. But being stubbornly determined, he soon joined the ranks of "first flight."[3]

One has to wonder, while fox hunting, did he wear his Western garb, with a stampede strap to keep his hat on and yell "yahoo" like a buckaroo, or did he dress in a traditional red hunting uniform with a black top hat and call out "tally-ho?" Either way, it certainly would have amused his crusty cowboy cronies in Jackson had they witnessed it.

In New York, he stayed with a famous portrait painter who had been a frequent Bar BC client. His patron gave a dinner in Cal's honor and put him next to a worldly French Countess who was famous for her decadent leanings. Cal thought she was the "...nicest, simplest...little woman he had ever become acquainted with." Struthers Burt later commented, "Cal had a way with women."[4]

On an earlier occasion, a famous blond-haired motion picture actress, Mary Miles Minter, was in Jackson for the filming of *The Cowboy and the Lady*. At a gathering where the starlet was being patronizingly gracious to "the dear simple people [of Jackson]," she learned a local greeting. Bubbling, she asked Cal, "How did you winter?" "Fine," he replied, "I wintered in Paris, Berlin, and Rome."[5]

In the 1920s, after Cissy had married Elmer Schlesinger and sometime before his Africa hunting trip, Cal met a woman named Goldie Chisman who lived at 3765 Fifth Avenue, San Diego. She and Cal carried on a correspondence and friendship

Cal Carrington with poodle, tea cup and silk socks at Cissy's mansion
in Washington, D.C., c early 1940s.
Courtesy of Joe Arnold and family.

for thirty years, up until Cal's passing. At first their letters indicated a romance; later, friendship. Goldie would visit and sometimes stay at Cal's ranch in Driggs when he was away.

In one of her letters Goldie wrote, "I remember how beautiful the lilacs and poppies were on the road to your place, one spring." Cal replied from Jackson, July 1928, "I just got your letter so I can go home [to Driggs] contented. You did not say you maid it home when we left...everything was all right when I came back...I ben so lon som every since, all I live for it to come and see you again [in San Diego]."[6]

After Felicia moved to New York, she said, "Cal would take a train East and find his way to my walkup apartment on 35th Street off Park Avenue, simply by remembering the convolutions of the land...I'd hear a knock on the door, and there would be this loveable, silver-haired giant in his cowboy boots and ten-gallon hat...He'd bring elk meat that he'd roast in my apartment fireplace for me and my friends."[7]

Earlier, Cissy had described, "...for all his lithe slimness, he was well along in years."[8] It was true; by this time Cal was getting up in years, but he was still a vigorous man.

I Always Did Like Horses & Women

20
Teton Valley Roots

"We believe the entire Jackson Hole should be set aside as a recreation area,"[1] was how a 1925 petition signed by ninety-seven Jackson Hole residents read. The petitioners, however, were not as altruistically motivated as might first appear. Rather they were hopeful the government would buy them out and relieve them of their hardscrabble existence. Charlie Peterson, Sr., referred to homesteading in Jackson Hole in those years as "a living dug out of the rocks."[2] People were tired of back-breaking labor, sub-zero temperatures, rutabagas and game meat.

But the petitioners hardly represented a unanimous opinion. Throughout the 1920s and into the 1940s the Hole's residents were bitterly divided among themselves as to which direction the valley's future should take. While Teton National

Park was first dedicated in 1929, certain prominent Wyoming ranchers and families remained staunchly opposed to it. In Jackson, they enlisted movie actor Wallace Beery on their side to gain national attention. Moreover, they tried to paint individuals who favored Park designation, such as Struthers Burt, Mardy and Olaus Murie, and the Rockefellers, as extremists—the radical environmentalists of the time.[3] In the end, after years of local and legislative attacks opposing it, Grand Teton National Park as we know it was finally established in 1950.

Over that time period the inevitable winds of change swept through the Hole. Cal's friend and oldtimer Frank Peterson died in 1929, others left or moved on. By the 1930s, most of the homestead ranches on the Elk Refuge had faded from the scene, and the private in-holdings within the Park gradually followed over the next few decades, all being acquired by the government. Where Cal came down on the issue isn't known, but we might assume he was politic about expressing his opinions.

The Depression of the 1930s and World War II came and went without much change in lifestyle for those who hung on in the Hole. Ranching and eking out subsistence went on pretty much as before. Oldtimer Roy Chambers, who was born at Grovont (Mormon Row) north of Jackson, summed it up: "We never realized there was a Depression because we were living on the ranch and had no money anyway. But we always had enough to eat."[4]

Dude ranching and outfitting were the primary sources for any cash money. Budget travelers who came to the Hole and couldn't afford the top-dollar dude ranches were disparagingly referred to as "tin-can tourists." Cal was in the gravy compared to most in those lean years. Cash was a scarce commodity, but he was receiving a monthly stipend from Cissy. Her ranch and personal expenditures were a one-person booster to the local economy.

In 1929, Cissy had furniture shipped to the ranch. A piano, and other items, including a large couch, were hauled by horse and wagon from the railhead at Victor over Teton Pass, and then up the narrow wagon road to the ranch by ox cart. The skilled wagon crews that accomplished this feat earned their pay, but were happy there was any money to be made at all. Nowadays, Flat Creek Ranch guests look at the piano and couch, which are still in use in the lodge, and shake their heads in wonderment. The thought of moving them, especially a piano, up the narrow, bumpy road to the ranch by ox-drawn wagon seems like an impossible and heroic feat.

Long-time Jackson resident Johnny Ryan claimed, "Cal liked to help people out, and in those days there was plenty a needin' help." Johnny recalled one homesteader who was having a hard time: "Cal made it a point to ride out there and tell 'im: 'I got twenty dollars, I don't need it; here, I'll just give it to you.' "[5]

Toward the end of this period, Cal reconnected with Teton Valley. He became more involved with farming his 160 acres at Bates, growing hay and ninety-day oats, and in addition to running up to twenty-five head of cattle he also raised hogs and chickens. When he was gone from Teton Valley, he arranged for his neighbors to look after his place and livestock.[6]

In late winter 1931, Cal did just that: left his livestock in care of his neighbors, and he and a friend toured northern Arizona—Prescott, Jerome, Williams, Flagstaff and the Grand Canyon—by automobile. They visited the Hoover Dam site where construction had gotten underway in September 1930. Carrington had a knack for being at historical Western crossroads and witnessing things for himself. The dam is considered one of the greatest engineering works in history. It took five years to complete and transformed the American Southwest. The trip involved nearly a month; Cal didn't return until the first week in April, after the snow had receded from the Valley.[7]

In July, after things had settled down from his tour of the Southwest, Cal wrote Goldie from the Crabtree Hotel in Jackson. "Loks like I wont half to work at all this summer...Movies has gone a way...Just a stray Dude now and a gain...What do you do Sundays now days, tell me so I can doo just the opsit, I believe that is the way the sects [sexes] works."

Wrangling dudes and their horses in the heat of summer and packing hunters into cold snowy camps began to be a job best left to the young bucks. Besides, as former Wyoming Senator Cliff Hansen remembers, "Cissy's good friend, Rose Crabtree, had taken a proprietary interest in the Flat Creek Ranch for her."[8] Cal didn't need to be there all that much, and apparently Cissy didn't want him there either. Cissy hired Forney Cole to caretake the ranch. Hansen believed Forney was the best horseman he ever knew. He was also rumored to be "the toughest man in Jackson" and, much to Cissy's disgust, "the dirtiest and most in need of a bath."

However, based on a story former Museum Director Bob Rudd recalls about Forney, he did sometimes wash his clothing. On one occasion, Forney put his clothing in the washing machine at the ranch, then forgetting about them, went into Jackson. The next day when he returned, "they were still washing, but only threads and buttons remained."[9]

While at the ranch Forney gained notoriety by fighting off a bear attack with a club. The club Forney used, and a national newspaper article detailing how he beat the bruin off of him, are framed and still on display at Dornan's Bar in Moose, Wyoming.

Regardless, Cal still felt obligated to make occasional trips over to Jackson to check on things, satisfying himself that everything at the ranch was in good order. To say Cal and Forney "bristled at each other" was an understatement. Cissy's biographer Martin wrote, "In a showdown, Forney told Cal, 'By God, one of us better go, and it ain't a gonna be me.'" Forney had a speech impediment, so perhaps he didn't articulate it as well as Martin described it, nevertheless, the point was made. The story goes, "Cal laughed, but left."[10]

Cal's own version in a July 1931 letter to Goldie is a bit different: "The countes had a lot of foundations put under her cabans, and I went up thaire and got teh men all sore at me...but believe they got through quicker. the Watchman [however,] said he was going to quit..." The "Watchman" was caretaker Forney.

Although electricity was widely available in Teton Valley after 1923 from a plant located in the Teton River canyon, some believe that Cal lived at Bates without benefit of modern conveniences. He used kerosene lamps and candles for light. He had no indoor plumbing, his water came from a rain barrel and a spring or shallow well he had dug near the cabin. In winter, he melted snow.

A woodstove heated the cabin and also served for cooking. If he needed a telephone, he went over to the Furniss homestead next door. His Mormon neighbors in Teton Valley, for whom family was all-important, thought of Cal as "alone in the world without anyone to depend on;" "...a lone man;" "...a solitary man;" "...a hermit;"[11] and we might add, a character of sorts.

Cal would turn heads by going into Driggs wearing chaps and spurs.[12] At one time cowboy regalia wasn't even noticed in Teton Valley, and in Jackson it still didn't attract a second glance, but among the servants of the soil in Teton Valley, it caused sidelong glances. Still, in that community of, by then, second- and third-generation ranchers and farmers, Cal received the unconditional respect granted to oldtimers. After all, he had come into the Valley when it was still the frontier, and his generation was cherished as proof of the pioneering past.

When Mormon men went into Driggs, they generally did not carouse in a bar, instead they visited the barbershop. The local blather got passed around there. Cal generally dropped in on the barbershop when he was in town, entertaining everyone with his yarns. The barbershop crowd would try to get him to talk about the Countess,[13] straining forward for any tasty morsel like tethered hounds at feeding time. However, while Cal expounded on farming, hunting, rodeo, horses, and places he had traveled, he remained gentlemanly unforthcoming about the Countess. He felt it was "none of their damn business."

George Furniss had the homestead immediately south of Carrington's, and Cal would go over to the Furniss farm occasionally to get milk and eggs. Oren Furniss, George's son, was a stereotypical farm boy, complete with straw hat, overalls, and chewing on a piece of timothy. Cal was a curiosity to him, fueled no doubt from overhearing the adult chatter about their bachelor neighbor. Oren and Cal became good friends.[14]

On occasion, Cal invited the neighbor children—Oren Furniss, Farrell Buxton, Monty Piquet and others—over to his cabin to see his African souvenirs and hear his tales. "I liked to listen to his stories," Oren said, "and he had all kinds of trinkets to show us."

Cal, of course, ever the consummate raconteur, took pleasure in telling his tales, delighting in the wide-eyed astonishment he could engender among the local farm kids: "He had a rhinoceros horn mounted on a board," and best of all, "He'd swat flies with a swatter made from an elephant's tail while he talked."[15]

Cal employed Oren to help him cultivate his fields. In planting ninety-day oats, Oren would drive a team of horses pulling a wagon up and down the field while Cal sat with a tub of loose grain between his knees and broadcast seed by hand. Oren emphasized, "Cal was a strict taskmaster. Everything had to be done exactly as he wanted, especially keeping the rows straight. For a day's work, Cal paid me one dollar."[16]

One time, Oren was across the ditch, where Cal couldn't see him, when a rooster crowed. Oren remembered Cal shouting at the rooster, "What in the hell do you have to crow about?"

As Oren got older and was working in his family's fields plowing and cultivating, he fondly recalls "Cal would step outside his cabin at exactly 11:30 and wave a white flag, signaling lunch was ready, then I'd go have lunch with him."[17]

Cal must have gotten electricity installed into his cabin at some point, because he purchased what was in those days called "talking furniture" – a radio. But when he went to use his "radio setup," he said it would "only growl at him." Next his "word machine" (typewriter) gummed up. Ever resourceful, he used coal oil (kerosene) to clean it. For some time afterward though his letters reeked of a curious odor, as if they had originated from a petroleum refinery.[18]

At some point, too, Cal kept a Model T Ford at his Bates Ranch. Apparently, it was frustratingly temperamental about starting. Cal complained to a neighbor, "I cranked her 'til she boiled."[19]

Sometimes it did get lonely at the Bates Ranch, too. In January 1938, Cal wrote Goldie, "Thanks for the Xmas card. Why didn't you tell me how many bows you have and stur me up a little...I haven't had a girl smile at me for so long, I wouldn't believe it was me if they did...coming down [to San Diego] to see you some day soon.[20]

21

Hard Knocks

Cal rightfully took pride in his horsemanship, so when a cranky little horse he was riding on his Bates ranch—a horse he had disparagingly named "Scrubby" because of its size—began bucking for whatever reason, Cal stubbornly stayed with him. Cal, however, was in his late sixties and no longer an agile young cowboy. Before it was over, Scrubby, with sky-hopping maneuvers the infamous bucking horse, Steamboat, would have admired, managed to pitch Cal violently onto the saddlehorn.[1]

In that painful hoofed incident the self-esteem from a lifetime of working with dangerous stock without serious injury was ruefully besmirched by the little horse. Remounting Scrubby, while cursing him thoroughly, Cal struggled back to his cabin, refusing to see a doctor. Oren Furniss recalled, "Cal was down for ten days recovering from the injury, while neighbors looked in on him and helped out."[2]

Then another accident followed a few years later while gathering his winter supply of firewood. Firewood was an annual necessity, and it involved a lot of labor back then— hitching up and driving a horse-drawn wagon into the forest; using a single-buck, cross-cut saw and double-bit axe to fell and cut the trees into lengths; then loading the wood onto the wagon and hauling it down the mountain. It was honest hard work, and Cal had been doing it for years. It was an accustomed autumn chore in the high mountain valleys surrounding the Tetons. But sometimes even experienced hands have accidents and working alone makes it more risky. Anyone in Teton Valley who has ever heard of Cal Carrington generally knows the story of his near fatal wood-hauling mishap.[3]

Cal had cut a large wagonload of wood in October of 1943. It was late in the day when he started down out of Middle Twin Creek with it. Sitting sideways on the load, he was driving his old bay horse teamed with a new horse he had recently purchased from Frank Moss, the local forest ranger at Driggs. Perhaps Cal's mind wandered, but suddenly on a steep downgrade, the new horse picked up his gait and the bay followed. Sitting sideways on the load, Cal found himself unable to gain any leverage to check them. As the horses ran down the mountain trail, the wagon hit a rut, bouncing and pitching Cal forward. He went down between the wagon tongue and the horses, and the wheels of the heavily loaded wagon ran over him, badly breaking his left arm and right leg.

It was a serious situation. He was alone, both bones protruded through the flesh on his arm, his leg was numb and useless. It was one and a half miles down the wagon road to the closest neighbor (five miles from his own cabin), night was coming on, the temperature was dropping, and the horses and wagon were gone. Cal had experienced severe challenges before in his life and he didn't panic. He rolled to the center of the road and onto his left side, and with the help of his right arm, began crawling down the canyon.

After an interminable length of time he reached the forest boundary where the gate had stopped the team. It was all he could do to open the gate and he realized he wouldn't be able to get himself up onto the wagon or handle the reins. It occurred to him that he could turn the team loose and send them down the canyon. Someone seeing the unhitched team would know there had been trouble and come up to investigate.

Straining with difficulty, he crawled and struggled around under the traces until he was able to get them undone. Then wiggling out to the side of the new horse, he smacked it on the rump. The team moved off but only went a short way down the road before turning off into the trees.

There was no alternative but to continue to seesaw his way down the road as he had been doing before. His badly broken arm kept getting in the way of his good one. He managed to get a piece of barbed wire loose from a fence and improvise a sling by twisting it around the wrist of the helpless arm and hooking the other end through his shirt collar.

In this manner, foot by exhausting foot, he worked his way down the road until 1:00 a.m. when he reached neighbor Fred Bowen's barnyard. It was dark in the house, but with all the energy he could muster, he called out, "Fred, come and get me."

The Bowens heard the call as they lay in bed and figured it was a drunk. Fred took his time dressing. When he finally went out and turned his light on the form lying in the barnyard muck, he recognized Cal Carrington.

It was impossible for Fred to get Cal into the house alone. He sent his wife, Rula, to get a neighbor. Between all of them, they finally managed to get Cal into the house and cleaned the dirt and barnyard muck off of him. They attended to Cal the rest of the night. He was not in shock and didn't complain.

Early in the morning Merlin Christensen and Cal's neighbor, George Furniss, arrived with a car, and all of them working together loaded Cal up and drove him to the hospital at Idaho Falls. Cal's postscript to it all was that he refused to be taken to the hospital until, with assistance, he had shaved, bathed and was dressed in borrowed clothes: "I wasn't a-goin' to let no pretty young Mormon nurses see me in no shape like that," he said. Struthers Burt later commented, "Cowboys can be vain."4

After three weeks, they could not make him stay in the hospital any longer, and within four months, he was back at work. Remarkable for a man of any age and Cal was seventy! As historian Gillette put it, "The incredible man, Carrington, was repaired with no noticeable impairments." Fred Bowen remarked: "Cal was rugged, tough and determined, both mentally and physically."

However, the back-to-back accidents caused Cal to reflect on his mortality, because on October 13, 1941, he secretly made out and recorded a warranty deed in Driggs for the sale of his Bates property to Eleanor Patterson for one dollar.5 He never told Cissy or anyone about it, but it was there in the record book for when he died.

Why would he deed his property over to Cissy? The unorthodox and curious conveyance of his property outside of a will was typical of the unconventional way he had conducted business most of his life. It almost makes one smile. He no doubt chuckled to himself while doing it, picturing Cissy's annoyance when she learned of it. But it may also say something about their long-term relationship and his feelings of indebtedness towards her, too. No doubt he intended it as some kind of final statement to her.

After his accidents had brought him face to face with his mortality, he must have figured he'd die before Cissy, who was six years younger; but it wasn't to be the case.

22

Cissy's Passing

In writing about Jackson Hole, Cissy once confided, "I have seen taller mountains and larger lakes, but the people I love."[1]

In 1948, while in residence at her Dower Estate in Maryland, she knew she was dying and asked for her private railroad car to be prepared to take her to Jackson Hole one last time. She never made it. She passed away in her sleep on July 24. Fourteen years had gone by since she had last visited Jackson. During that time, she had been consumed with high-level politics and running a publishing empire. Her estate at the time of her death was estimated at sixteen million dollars.

Cissy had, however, continued correspondence with her good friend Rose Crabtree for all those years. Once she arranged for Rose and Henry to visit her in Washington. She asked Rose what she'd like to see. Rose half-jokingly replied, "I'd like to meet the president." Cissy had it arranged and Rose met President William Taft, a friend of the Patterson family.[2]

When Rose learned of Cissy's death, she cried. Cal had taken a trip over to the Salmon River two weeks earlier, fell asleep while driving home and went off the road and rolled his vehicle. He was hospitalized with bruises and broken ribs: "sore and sorry," as he put it. News of Cissy's passing reached him the day before he got out of the hospital. He was struck quiet, then he muttered sadly, "If only we could have had one more trip together."[3] A fine old friendship was gone. He later wrote Goldie, "I certainley feal the loss of the Countis."[4]

Cissy's passing unsettled him. Following her death, it was not a coincidence that he became embroiled in a number of quarrelsome issues.[5] He didn't dwell on his feelings, "that's just the way things was," but in truth, he became cantankerous and maybe a bit morose. Cissy left the entire Flat Creek Ranch property to her cousin Josephine Patterson Albright. Josephine found Flat Creek Ranch too remote for her liking and consigned it to caretakers and renters.

Another reason Cal may have been upset, Cissy had not willed him any part of the Flat Creek Ranch. It was a blow that tormented him. After all, the Flat Creek Ranch and canyon had been a big piece of his life for many years, going back to at least 1901 and, too, he felt it had been his doings that had gotten title to the property in the first place. He must have felt somewhat further betrayed since, after all, in what maybe he imagined was a conspiratorial pact, he had deeded over his Bates property to her if he should die first.[6]

On lonely nights, while winds shrilled in the stovepipe and gloom crept down from the Big Hole Mountains behind his dark cabin, he obsessed about the fact that Cissy used to call the Flat Creek Canyon trapper's cabin, where he had often stayed in the early years, *his cabin*. Rummaging around in his trunk, under shadowy light cast by a kerosene lamp, he found an old letter where she had off-handedly referred to it in that manner—"his cabin."[7]

It was evidence enough for Cal. It proved to him Cissy intended the cabin, and six acres they had once talked about, to be *his*. The fact she hadn't mentioned it in her will—well, that was mere oversight in his mind.

Cal sought legal assistance, initiating a lawsuit. In building his case, he retrieved his 1922 Flat Creek homestead patent from his trunk where he had kept it all those years. He finally recorded it, long after the fact, in Jackson on July 24, 1953,[8] to strengthen his case. But his legal wrangling went cussedly slow and was to no avail.

He traveled back to New York to enlist Felicia's help on the lawsuit. By this time, he had worked himself into a self-righteous wrath. He exclaimed to Felicia, coming down hard on the last word, "...the cabin and six acres, they're *mine!*" She wisely put him off, telling him, "We'll talk about it in the morning."[9]

Not easily deterred, Cal returned to Jackson and moved into the old Flat Creek cabin, obstinately taking up residence, working old tricks: taking possession, squatter's rights, claim jumping, bluffing and blustering. Cal was of the school that believed possession was proof of ownership, an opinion born from his frontier years.

Al Remington's patience, to whom Josephine was leasing the ranch, quickly grew thin from the quarrelsome run-ins. Al called the sheriff out and Cal was evicted. "It was the only time in my life," Cal fumed, "that a sheriff ever caught up with me."[10]

Afterward, in a letter that indicated he truly believed he had a legal interest in the cabin, Cal wrote Josephine Patterson Albright:

Dear Friend..., Mr. Remington...got the sheriff and run me off; broke in [to the cabin] and took possession...If i sew him for rent, would it inter fear with your plans, he sais he would have a damage suit against you...I want one hundred dollars a month [rent] during the life of his leas...he is doing no good up theair...[11]

Times had changed in Jackson Hole, the frontier code wherein a man could have whatever he wanted—as long as he was strong enough to take it—no longer prevailed. In spite of all the legal wrangling that went on over Cissy's will, though, Cal continued to hold onto the ideal that she had wanted him to have the cabin and six acres. He stubbornly continued to occasionally visit and stay at the Flat Creek cabin. In fact, his last time there was in May of 1959, only months before his death.[12] Perhaps he visited there out of nostalgia, remembering the old times.

Around the same time, Cal also became caught up in water right disputes and meetings with his Teton Valley neighbors. If someone is looking to pick a fight in the West, water rights are always a good starting place. As Mark Twain said, "Whiskey is for drinkin'; water is for fightin'." Teton Valley native Farrell Buxton, who recalls Cal's remonstrations says, "As a youngster, I tried to avoid the frequent meetings and long arguments about water that went on."[13]

Cal had a recorded water right on Mahogany Creek in Teton Valley, filed on May 26, 1900 and again in 1901, but he

Driggs Idaho   Aug   5/1952

        Mrs, Allbright
        Dear Friend

The U.S.Destrict Cort
in Washington,D,C,

Alowed me A cabin and a few acers on
Flat Creek Medows,not deaded but as
a Intrest,
Mr ,Remington your Laser got the sherif
and run me off,,broke in and took poshen
If i sew him for rent,would inter fear
with your plans,he sais he would have a
damage suit a gainst you,
If you dont claim my Cabin ,it looks to
me he wouldent get verey for,
I would like your Lowyer-tety--to take
my cace on a comishan forwhat he colects,
I want one hundred dallars a month during
the life of his leas,
he is dooing no good up theair,taks his
doods up a fishing,Killed of all the Beavers
this last year,
I was theair a while in July ,saw no in
provements what so ever,more harm than good,
If you and your Lowyer dont like my butting
in pleas tell me,
Eney advice I would like to have it,from
you, I stick a round worts Hotel when in
Jackson,look me up when you are theair,
            As ever your Friend,
                    Carrington
            Driggs Idaho

Cal Carrington's 1952 letter to Josephine (Patterson Reeve) Albright
regarding the disposition of the Flat Creek Ranch.
Courtesy of Flat Creek Ranch.

Cal Carrington in Jackson, Wyoming, at age 82.
Courtesy of JHHSM, 1958.0022.001P.

sometimes had trouble getting his share of the water. "First in time, first in right" is the decree. But in practice, by the time those above him took off water in late summer, little reached his place since he was at the bottom end of the ditch. Water coming down the ditch needed to be "divided in the field," requiring cooperation among neighbors.

Conversely, his neighbor Oren Furniss's wife, Eva, expressed appreciation for Cal's efforts which assisted them in obtaining water they needed for their farm.[14] Still, neighborly cooperation generally wasn't forthcoming from Cal in those years. Teton Valley rancher Art Mackley said, "Carrington enjoyed being an authoritative know-it-all and tried to assert himself over others with threats, bluffs, and deceptive mannerisms to gain the upper hand."[15]

Cal fomented on the water issue, deciding he was going to single-handedly resolve the situation. But the problem of his disputed water rights may have been more complicated. Any early established right which had not been used for more than five years was subject to preemption by a "prescriptive right" filing, and another rancher made such a filing on Cal's rights, hiring attorney Harold Forbush to prepare the claim and give Cal notice by letter.[16]

Next, Cal resurrected an old grievance with the Crabtrees. Rose had the angora chaps he had long ago given to Cissy. Nobody wore angora chaps anymore and Cal couldn't have possibly had any use for them; they would never have fit him. He wanted them back for sentimental reasons, they were a tangible part of his past. Once again, Cal asked— "pesticated" as he called it—Felicia to intervene for him, insisting Cissy had wanted him to have the chaps. "They're mine!" he'd complain.

Rose responded pithily: "Tell him if he's real good, I'll bury him in them."[17]

Today the chaps are part of the Jackson Hole Museum's collection.

Next, the county sent Teton Valley resident Russell Stone and his crew to contour an embankment along Cal's property line for a road and a fence location. Cal distrusted their ability to do a good job and carefully monitored the progress. However, he liked the completed work.

It was a hot and dusty day, so Cal brought out a case of beer to share. Russell and his men, all devout Mormons, refused the beer. Cal was offended. Russell said, "He walked away and never spoke to me again, not ever."[18] The incident recalls what Struthers Burt once described: "without a word of explanation...sharp as moonlight, cold as a knife."

"Cal," Felicia said to him, "why don't you quit that foolishness about suing everyone and fighting with your neighbors?" He was quiet for a while, then burst out, "Girl, I'm too old to ride in any more rodeos. I can't steal no more horses. Your Mama is gone. My God, I've got to find something that is entertainin'."[19]

23

The Jeep and Encinitas

Sometime after World War II, Cal had gotten himself a green Willys Jeep. He would bounce over Teton Pass to Jackson in no time, compared to the long and arduous trips over the same route on horseback or by wagon that he had known in the past.

Unlike his earlier hot-headed and reckless driving with the Countess's Ford truck, now instead, he'd occupy the middle of the road holding everyone up. Passengers who rode with him would joke and complain: "Hey, go over that bump again, my head ain't come off yet."[1]

He and his neighbor, George Furniss, would drive up to the Salmon River to fish for Chinook salmon and be gone several days. They'd return, Oren remembered, with salmon that would "stretch across the hood of the jeep; other times they would go to Jackson Lake ice fishing."[2]

Even though Cal had the jeep, at first he still kept and used horses, too. If you were a horseman all your life, you didn't give it up quickly, in spite of motor cars and other mechanized contraptions. Oldtimers like Cal always had a distrust of mechanical things. After all, "Horses," they'd say, "started more dependably than engines." At some point, though, Cal rarely stayed in Teton Valley in the winter. And he gave up all his livestock and horses.

When winter came and snow began to drift around the cabin, he would catch a Greyhound bus from Driggs to his Encinitas, California, property, where he'd stay until spring when the snow in the valley had receded. Cal became a "snowbird."[3] He wasn't alone. His friend Jess Wort, for example, was also spending winters in southern California during that same time period.

When Cal applied for a permit to build on his Encinitas property, it was rejected. The house he proposed was too small under the zoning requirements. After mulling it over, he cleverly resubmitted the plans as a "garage." Tradition claims Cal built and lived in what was permitted as his garage.[4]

In September 1952, Cal wrote Goldie from New York, where he was visiting Felicia, "Hope to be along [to San Diego] some tim[e] this fall and get out of the coald."[5]

Cal's colorful personality and eccentricities caught people's attention. Teton Valley native Farrell Buxton recalled, "Cal worried someone would vandalize his cabin in Bates when he was gone, so he'd rig up a booby trap which released a spear toward the door when it was opened." No one, however, as far as is known, was ever impaled attempting to enter his cabin.[6]

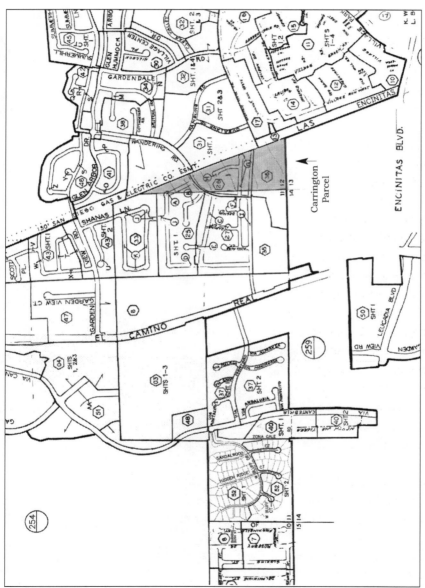

The shaded area shows where Cal Carrington's twenty-seven-acre parcel was located in Encinitas, California.

24

Felicia Returns to Jackson

Imagine what Cal must have thought about the contrast between revved-up southern California in the 1950s and Teton Valley, where some claim he still didn't even have electricity,[1] and the outhouse was out back; a place where, as Felicia noted, "He lived so poorly, he'd wear his clothing until it fell off him." Simply put, Cal chose to live alone in relative squalor at Bates, rather than spend his savings.

When he returned from California after the winter, one of the barbershop crowd in Driggs quipped, "It must be spring, the sandhill cranes and Cal Carrington are back." The witticism became a favorite around Driggs. Locals still recall it.[2]

Felicia's self-imposed exile from Jackson Hole had lasted until she was fifty years old. She had finally gained control over her alcohol problem. Cissy had been gone for many years. Cal was by then about seventy-nine years old and Felicia admitted, she "...felt doubt and hesitation about returning," but Rose Crabtree wired her saying, "You are as welcome as the flowers in spring."[3]

Jackson was no longer a frontier town with hitching posts, livery stables and the clomping of cowboy boots on wooden boardwalks. Cal's long-time friends, the Crabtrees, sold their landmark hotel in 1952. Trees and grass had been planted in the dusty square in the 1940s and the first elk antler arch was erected by 1953.

Cal had told Felicia about the changes in Jackson Hole over the years when he visited New York: "There's a park where the square used to be...big paved roads where motor cars kin go...the Park Service has people stayin' in camps and motels where they can't git lost...you can git to town without gettin' tangled in sagebrush...they's got all kinda lookin' people in big crowds on the streets and all kinda things in them new stores."[4]

After Felicia arrived in Jackson, Cal rented some gentle horses and they rode up Cache Creek. Then on another day, they trucked horses over to Flat Creek and rode up the old wagon road into the canyon and toward the ranch. Felicia wrote, they "rode up to a fence with a padlocked gate, where Cal dismounted and said, 'Here, hold my horse.' "[5]

Still resentful about the disposition of the Flat Creek Ranch property, and in spite of Felicia's protests, Cal proceeded to break down the fence. The ranch was leased to Al Remington at the time, who was also the owner of the Wagon Wheel in Jackson. Cal wasn't about to be locked out of the ranch which he had considered his for many years, and a part of which he still felt belonged to him. When they encountered the ranch manager, he took Cal aside, threatening, "If you ever come back I'll get the sheriff and have you jailed."[6]

They continued on their ride, Cal taking Felicia straight up the old trail towards Sheep Mountain, the same way he and Cissy used to ride decades before. Felicia said, "Cal was muttering to himself and shaking his fist the whole time...all he was thinking about was that Remington wouldn't let him go back to his cabin and six acres."[7]

Amazingly, though, at that age, Cal apparently still retained his skill in the mountains, the same ability Struthers Burt had been impressed with years before, because Felicia recorded: "He got back [to the horse trailer] the way an animal gets home— straight through the country, right on target."[8]

It's known Cal spent time at the cabin in early spring 1951; he wrote Goldie about it: "I took a stroal to the upper end of the field and I bumped into a big black bear..." And again, for the last time, in spring of 1959, when he wrote Felicia: "[I] locked it up and naild a sine on [the] door, 'Keep Out.'" That was the last mention of anyone seeing the old Flat Creek cabin. Whatever became of the cabin after that time, no one today knows. It was either accidentally or purposely burned down.

Present-day ranch owner Joe Albright reports, "There are remnants of an old cabin that burned some unknown time in the past. In the dirt at that location we found pieces of an iron stove with a mid-1800s date."[9]

The present-day location of the gate at the Flat Creek Ranch property boundary may, or may not, have been the actual spot used by horse thieves to shut off the canyon more than a century ago. More likely, it was down at the bottom of the meadows.

Cal's last horse pack trip was taken with Felicia to Two Ocean Pass on the Continental Divide, deep within what is today's Teton Wilderness. John and Jess Wort outfitted them. This was country where Cal used to outfit and guide hunters, and he knew it well. He confided to Felicia they were close to where he had taken Cissy on their first hunting trip over forty years before.[10]

Anyone who has made the trip into Two Ocean Pass can appreciate it as a long and demanding horseback ride. Incredibly, Cal was eighty-three years old. Felicia says, "He still rode magnificently, and around camp still moved with a grace that an Eastern man never has."[11] On the trail, it recalled an earlier time, when Cal would call back over his shoulder: "For God's sake, kick that horse of yours, and come on!"

25

A Cowboy's Last Years

Cal leased out his farmland in Bates in the 1950s and generally retired to Encinitas in the winters. Jack Buxton was a lessee for several years in the 1950s, and later, Jack Spencer had the ground. Farrell and Jaydell, Jack Buxton's sons, remember putting up hay in Cal's field. Farrell said, "We used side delivery rakes and baled the hay, then sold it to a feed lot at Sugar City."[1]

Orville "Jack" Buxton and his boys would go to Cal's cabin and visit with him. Farrell recalls, he and Jaydell would sit on the edge of Cal's rough-built bunk, fascinated, while "Cal spun yarns about Africa." Farrell also remembers Cal's rhinoceros horn mounted on a board. And him swatting flies with the "elephant's tail," while moving about like an actor on stage telling his tales. Africa was an unimaginably distant place to Teton Valley farmers in those days.

Farrell recalled on one occasion when he was approaching Cal's cabin, Cal was trying to comb his hair flat, but "he had a rooster-tail that kept sticking up. Cal didn't know I was there and he was cussing up a blue thunderbolt."[2]

There's no doubt Cal was an original character. Those who met him did not forget him. Evidence points to him being more than a bit ornery in his later years, too. Interestingly, Cissy was considered to be something of a misanthrope in her later years, as well. Local lore claims she, like Cal, was accomplished at the art of cussing. One teamster on the Pass, who considered himself adept in the art of cussing, claimed, "Cissy was the only other person he let talk to his horses when they needed talking to."[3] In some ways, on certain levels, Cal and Cissy were a matched pair.

Oldtimers who had lived through having to make every meager bit count just to get by, sometimes revert to the same parsimonious behavior in their later years, whether they need to or not. Such was the case with Cal. Maybe, too, it was what the strict Mormon elder had ingrained into Cal as a child. In any case, Farrell remembered Cal would get a pitchfork and go around the field complaining and picking up any small amount of missed hay. Farrell recalled, "It was hard to please Cal."

In those days, saloons were still more than just watering holes, they were places where the local news and gossip got circulated. When Cal was in Jackson he would invariably go to the Wort Hotel to visit his old sidekicks and share stories. As he put it: "I stick around Wort's Hotel when in Jackson."[4] Whenever Cal walked through the bar past the card players he'd routinely remark to them, "Still a doin' it."[5] After the gambling was shut down, Cal said, "Jackson became a dead town."

Cal enjoyed celebrity status in Jackson. Trail Creek ranch manager Margaret "Muggs" Shultz remembers being at the Jackson Hole rodeo in the early 1950s when Cal was introduced to the crowd. Muggs said, "He appeared tall and carried himself very erect when he walked into the arena. After the customary tipping of his hat to the crowd and applause, he went behind the chutes."[6]

Felicia wrote, "In the last summers of his life, Cal would come over from Driggs and stay at the Elbo," a small dude ranch located on Ditch Creek north of Jackson. Felicia's friend Katie Starret from California owned the ranch. Felicia wrote, "We'd all try to get him to take a bath," and he'd say, "Don't send my clothes to the laundry, they steal everything."[7]

According to Felicia, during Cal's last years, "The cabin in Driggs [Bates] was a hovel that was never cleaned." It's no doubt true, since Cal generally put off spring cleaning until he got around to it. In April 1941, he wrote Goldie: "I havent cleand the hous yet, I don't think I will. It has more dirt in side than thear is outside, so I gess I will just clean the farm insted."[8]

The cabin contained a curious and eclectic collection: a home-built bunk, a Captain's chair, a large trunk with personal items, a wood-burning cook stove, his "talking furniture," a "word machine," African trophies, saddles and horse harnesses hanging from the wall, and a closet containing suits hanging next to Western work clothing.[9]

Still, even in his eighties, Cal epitomized the Western image. There was an unpretentious aura of the true Westerner about him. He was willing to let Felicia buy him new shirts and trousers, and "with his great silver mane, like Buffalo Bill's,"

Felica recorded, "he'd cause such a sensation in Jackson, she and Katie Starret felt they were out with a movie star."[10]

In the last years of Cal's life, a brother, Zeneiph J. Julin, and two sisters, also in advanced age by then, located him. The brother came to Driggs to see him and tell him that the family had reached Salt Lake City where the parents were buried and that for years they had all tried to find him. Cal's response was: "It's only because the grass is green and tall on my place that you're a'comin' round now."[11]

Felicia tried to convince Cal he should forgive them: "...your parents did you a good turn, when you really look at it. If you'd stayed with them, you'd never had this wonderful life. You'd never met mama and me."

Reflecting for a moment, he agreed, "That's true." Felicia thought she had convinced him, however, she should have known better. "But it weren't no doin' of theirs," he concluded.[12]

Cal didn't let it rest there, though, he followed up on his life long resentment against his family. In his Last Will and Testament, he included a section specifying: "I recite that in my lifetime a certain person or persons have sought to claim blood relationship with me, for the purpose, I presume, of inheriting my property. However, I herewith renounce and disclaim any such relationship, and declare that no part of my estate should go to such person, but as herein above mentioned should be distributed to those persons who have proved to be my friends, and who have given me comfort and companionship in my life."[13]

On January 14, 1956, Cal filed suit in Teton County, Idaho, District Court against "Eleanor Patterson, if alive, and/or if dead, and all unknown heirs" obtaining a decree quieting and regaining full title to his Bates property.[14]

Instrument #54230 ✓✗   IN THE DISTRICT COURT OF THE NINTH JUDICIAL DISTRICT OF THE
                              STATE OF IDAHO, IN AND FOR TETON COUNTY

E. C. CARRINGTON sometimes known as   )
ENOCK C. CARRINGTON,   )
                    Plaintiff   )
)
        vs.   )
)
ELEANOR PATTERSON sometimes known as   )
CISSY PATTERSON, if alive, and/or if   )
dead ALL UNKNOWN HEIRS AND DEVISEES OF ELEANOR)   DECREE QUIETING TITLE
PATTERSON, and ALL UNKNOWN OWNERS OF Lots 1 & 2 of)
Section 6, Township 4, N. Range 45 EBM, Teton County,)
Idaho; and also E½SE¼ Section 31 Township 5, N. Range)
45 EBM, Teton County, Idaho; and also: NE¼SW¼ and)
the NW¼SE¼ Section 32, Township 5, N Range 45 EBM,)
Teton County, Idaho.   )
                    Defendants   )

        This cause came on for hearing this 13 day of January 1956, before his honor Henry S. Martin, sitting
without a jury; the plaintiff appearing by counsel A. A. Merrill and the defendants did not appear either
in person or by counsel, and it appearing to the court that due proof was submitted and each and all of
the defendants were duly served with summons by publication as required by law and that each of said defendants have defaulted in said cause; that none thereof have answered or appeared herein within the time
allowed by law after service of summons as aforesaid or at all, and upon motion of counsel for the plaintiff
default of the defendants was duly filed and was by the court ordered entered and was entered.

        Whereupon the court proceeded to hear the proofs submitted in plaintiff's complaint from which it
appears:

        1. That the court has jurisdiction over the subject matter of this suit and over the parties hereto
and the right to grant the relief prayed for in plaintiff's complaint.

        2. That all material allegations of the plaintiff's complaint are true and were duly proven.

        3. That the plaintiff is entitled to have the title to the real estate described in plaintiff's
complaint quieted in him.

        WHEREFORE, IT IS ORDERED, ADJUDGED AND DECREED:

        That the defendants and neither of them have any right, title, interest or estate whatsoever in and to
the said land and property hereinafter described.

        That the title of plaintiff in and to the said hereinafter described premises is good and valid and
the title of the plaintiff herein is adjudged to be quieted against all claims of all of the defendants and
that said defendants and each of them and all persons claiming through or under them and all unknown heirs
and devisees of Eleanor Patterson, if deceased, and all unknown owners of the property hereinafter described
are hereby debarred from asserting any right, title or interest in or to said land and premises or any
part thereof adverse to the plaintiff.

        That the said premises are bounded and described as follows to-wit:

Lots 1 and 2 of Section 6, Township 4, North Range 45 EBM, Teton County, Idaho; and also:
E½SE¼ Section 31 Township 5, North Range 45 EBM, Teton County, Idaho; and also: NE¼SW¼
and the NW¼SE¼ Section 32, Township 5, North Range 45 EBM, Teton County, Idaho

Dated this 13th day of January, 1956.

                                        Henry S. Martin
                                        Henry S. Martin
                                        District Judge
        Filed for record at 15 minutes past 11 o'clock A.M. this 14 day of January 1956 and recorded in book
83 of Judgments, page 1, records of Teton County, State of Idaho.
                                        Dwight C. Stone, Recorder
                                        By Beth Zohner, Deputy

Decree to recover title to his Bates ranch in 1956,
after Cal secretly deeded it to Eleanor Patterson in 1941.

In his last years, people recognized Cal as a link to bygone eras and a living Jackson Hole legend. In 1957, prior to his election as Wyoming governor in 1962, Jackson Hole rancher Cliff Hansen drove Cal to the University at Laramie where he conducted a recorded oral interview with him in the presence of history department faculty.

Retired professor Gene M. Gressley, who at the time was new at the University, relates Cal put on an unforgettable performance that had everyone laughing so hard they had to stop the interview at times. At one point in the grandstanding, Cal, dressed in western shirt with a bolo tie, stood up on the table and did his well-practiced African routine—mimicking animals and their sounds, including elephants trumpeting and giraffes mating. [15]

Cal seized the opportunity to give his unabashed opinions on, and associate his name with historic figures A.A. Anderson, Hiram Chittenden, Teton Jackson, Dick "Beaver Tooth" Leigh, Charlie Russell, and many more. Dwight Stone's recorded interview of Cal, arranged by Harold Forbush, followed in Teton Valley a year later. Interestingly, some of the questions similar to what Cal had answered at the University of Wyoming about his early cowboy years, in Stone's interview he dodged, saying, "None of your damn business."

In the autumn of 1959, Cal didn't leave for Encinitas. He was not feeling well enough, nor was he capable of staying alone at his cabin in Bates. He submitted to an examination by Jackson's Dr. Larsen in September who noted: "Very bad breathing." Cal's health continued to deteriorate that autumn: pneumonia followed by two heart attacks and stomach ulcers.

Cal allowed himself to be hospitalized in Jackson. A few days later, a "preacher" walked into his room and piously asked, "Are you ready to join the Church and commit to God?" Cal angrily struggled out of bed cussing, wrestled into his clothing and walked out of the hospital. Back in Driggs, he checked into the hospital there, only to indignantly stomp out again when they forgot to bring him breakfast. Next, in desperation, he tried sweat baths and electrical shock treatments with a healer in St. Anthony. When he returned after a week, a friend took one look at him and told him flat out, "You look like hell," after which Cal checked into the Driggs hospital again.[16] Old cowboys are independent cusses and can make difficult patients.

Two years earlier, Russia's Sputnik had ushered in the space age, and it would only be four more years until men walked on the moon, but in Teton Valley, Cal was still living as if it were an earlier era. His cabin had only the old woodstove for heat and cooking, some believe no electricity at the time and no running water nor indoor plumbing, just an outhouse and chamber pot. It would have been challenging for even a healthy young person to have lived there under those conditions with Teton Valley's rigorous winters.

Cal fought a good last fight and although he tried to stay at his cabin, in the end it was too much for him. He finally moved into Driggs, renting a cabin at the Harris' Cabins Motel. Earl and Sadie Harris were concerned about him and looked after him. After a lifetime of being close-mouthed with his neighbors about his personal life, Cal finally opened up with Earl, who listened to his reminiscences and amazing tales.[17]

Cal went back into the Driggs hospital in December but did not improve. Realizing his condition was serious, he had a friend in Jackson—a Mrs. Johnson—notify Felicia: "He's awfully sick and says he wants you to know about his property." Mrs. Johnson rattled off a list of real property and financial assets to Felicia over the phone—a fortune for a cowboy like Cal.

Felicia's disbelieving response was, "He certainly is sick; his mind is gone."[18] Felicia, who was living in Washington, D.C., at the time, immediately made arrangements and traveled to Driggs.

Cal was conscious and still rational when Felicia arrived. He said to her, "You look tired, Little Fellar, come sit down on the bed." She had brought him slippers and he protested, "You ain't a gonna' start dudin' me up now."[19]

While she was in Driggs, Felicia learned Cal's true story from the Harris family and Cal's neighbors in Bates. She had been one of Cal's closest friends for many years, yet before that time she hadn't even known his real name was Enoch Julin, or that his family had given him up to Mormon missionaries. She pretty much only learned those things from people in Teton Valley, and Cal himself, near the very end of his life.[20]

Cal had always cultivated dual identities—the glamorous Wild West Jackson Hole persona and a Teton Valley resident. Jackson Hole folks apparently knew little about Cal's life as Teton Valley farmer and California snowbird. They recall only colorful images of an outlaw, cowboy, outfitter and dude wrangler.

An exception was his friend Struthers Burt, with whom Cal had been inclined to share some of his true history, albeit sometimes a bit embellished. In Teton Valley, most were unimpressed with flashy Jackson Hole stories. They judged Cal more as a neighbor and on his down-to-earth lifestyle. His two personas reflected place as well as personality.

Cal Carrington died from pneumonia at 10 a.m. on December 22, 1959, without his boots on, in a clean hospital bed. He was eighty-six years old. Earl Harris was present at his passing. In

Cal's heyday, life expectancy for a man was about forty-nine years. Cal had managed to live a rugged and active long life that far exceeded every expectation for the times.

The old buckaroo had witnessed incredible changes over his lifetime. He had known the freedom of the West's unsettled open range, and had lived the romantic life of a cowboy on long cattle drives. When he first came into the Teton country in 1897, it was still wild, mostly unsettled, frontier. He had known, lived and worked among old time outlaws and original settlers who populated the Hole back then. The town of Jackson didn't even exist then; he witnessed its beginnings and growth. He worked for the Forest Service and Yellowstone National Park in their historical infancy. And he saw cattle drives, horses, hitching racks and livery stables give way to the arrival of the railroads, modern highways, tourism, and the space age, all in the course of his life.

For burial, Felicia dressed him in his "best checked wool shirt, his favorite bolo-tie and his least worn out pants."[21] He made the familiar trip over Teton Pass and down the mountain switchbacks into Jackson Hole one last time. A long procession of chained-up vehicles followed in the fresh snow that had fallen that morning. His old friend Berger was undoubtedly in that cavalcade, as no doubt were Buxtons, Furnisses, Gillettes, Harrises, Thompsons and others. Teton Pass was a different place from when Cal had first crossed it more than sixty years before. A ski rope tow had been operating there for a number of years and the trip across the pass into Jackson was made in less than an hour.

After a service and reading of the twenty-third Psalm, *"...he maketh me to lie down in green pastures and leadeth me beside the still water...,"* Cal was buried in the Aspen

Cemetery on Snow King Mountain on Christmas Eve. At the large gathering of friends and neighbors from both Teton Valley and Jackson, Felicia sadly noted, "Their tears were as genuine as mine."[22]

Felicia passed away in 1999. She also lived to see tremendous changes in Jackson Hole, including a Kmart and McDonald's, as compared to the wide-open country when she first experienced it at age eleven in 1916, a time in which, she later fondly described, "[she and her friends] could race bareback... galloping across the sage...with only one rule: be home in time for dinner." She is buried next to Cal, the inscription on her monument reads: "Life Long Friend of Cal Carrington."

Jackson Hole Guide obituaries
December 24 and 31, 1959

Cal Carrington Dead; Funeral Thursday

Last rites will be held Thursday, December 24 at 10:30 at the Elks Club for Cal Carrington, 86, who died Tuesday at the Driggs hospital. Cal was a member of B.P.O.E. 1712.

He first came to Jackson Hole in 1889, and lived here for many years. He later bought a ranch in Teton Valley, Idaho, which has been his home since, although he still visited over here.

In 1927 he went on a big game hunt in Africa, where he brought down three elephants and several species of other game animals. Some of the heads adorn the walls of the Silver Dollar Bar at the Wort Hotel and always attract interest, especially among outsiders.

Cal was the subject of a story in *Readers Digest* some years ago by Struthers Burt, "The Most Unforgettable Character I Ever Knew."

He was widely known in our Valley, and very well-liked by all.

A telephone call from Felicia Macgruder,(sic) Tuesday, said that he passed away quietly. She had flown from Washington a few days ago to be at his bedside. For many years Cal worked for Felicia's mother on "The Countess' Ranch" on upper Flat Creek, and the two had been friends since Felicia was a little girl.

Further information about this fine old gentleman will appear next week.

LAST RITES HELD THURSDAY FOR "CAL" CARRINGTON, EARLY PIONEER

Funeral services were held at 10:30 a.m. Thursday for Enoch C. Carrington at the Elks Lodge with burial in the Jackson Cemetery.

Enoch C. Carrington, "Cal" as his friends knew him, passed away peacefully at the Teton Valley Hospital at Driggs, Tuesday morning, December 22 of complications incident to old age. He was 86 years old.

Born in Sweden February 10, 1873 he came to the United States at the age of five and grew up in southern Utah. Carrington never married and the names of his parents are unknown.

He came to Jackson Hole in 1889 (sic) and lived here for many years. In 1898 he took out a homestead desert claim in Idaho, where he wintered during later years. Mr. Carrington was one of the first forest rangers in Jackson Hole, where he spent the major part of his life.

He worked as a cattle drover, driving from the southwest to Canada, and in 1914 began working as a guide, a work for which he later became quite famed throughout the United States.

Carrington was considered one of the greatest guides and big game hunters in the West, a trait which helped considerably during a two year stint in Africa hunting big game.

One of the great originals of the Old West, Carrington was a man by himself. His colorful personality, marked by eccentricities, marked him as an ideal subject for writers. Katherine Burt wrote a novel about him and Struthers Burt wrote an article, "The Most Unforgettable Character I Have Met" for *Readers Digest*.

The Jackson Hole Courier obituary
Thursday, December 31, 1959

CAL CARRINGTON
DIED DEC. 22

Funeral services were held in Jackson at the Elks Lodge Thursday Dec. 24 at 10:30 a.m. for Cal Carrington, long time resident of Jackson Hole and Teton Basin.

Enoch C. Carrington, "Cal" as his friends knew him, passed away peacefully at the Teton valley Hospital, Tuesday morning, December 22 of complications incident to age. He was 86 years old.

Born February 10, 1873 he came to the United States at the age of five andgrew up in southern Utah. Carrington never married and the names of his parents are unknown. He is thought to have been born in Sweden.

He came to Teton Valley in April 1898, took out a homestead desert entry claim, where he frequently wintered during later years. Mr. Carrington was one of the first forest rangers in the Jackson Hole where he spent the major part of his life.

He worked as a cattle drover, driving from the southwest to Canada and in 1914 began working as a guide, a work for which he later became quite famed throughout the United States.

In 1914 he started work as a guide on a dude ranch in the Jackson Hole area. He became a guide for Mrs. Eleanor Patterson. She subsequently bought a ranch of his at Jackson Hole. He traveled extensively in Europe and did some big game hunting there.

Several articles have been written about the colorful life of Mr. Carrington. He was a member of the Elks Lodge in Jackson.

One of the great originals of the Old West, Carrington was a man by himself. His colorful personality marked by eccentricities mark him (sic) an ideal subject for writers. Katherine Burt wrote a novel about him and Struthers Burt an article "The Most Unforgettable Character I have Met" for *Readers Digest.*

Carrington was considered one of the greatest guides and big game hunters in the West, a trait which helped considerably during a two year stint in Africa hunting big game.

Teton Valley News obituary
Thursday, December 24, 1959

Funeral services will be held at 10:30 a.m. today (Thursday) for Enoch C. Carrington at the Elks Lodge in Jackson, Wyoming.

Enoch C. Carrington, "Cal" as his friends knew him, passed away peacefully at the Teton Valley Hospital, Tuesday morning, December 22 of complicaticns incident to old age. He was 56 years old.

Born in Sweden February 10, 1873, he came to the United States at the age of five and grew up in southern Utah. Carrington never married and the names of his parents is unknown.

He came into the valley in April 1898, took out a homestead desert claim, where he frequently wintered during later years. Mr. Carrington was one of the first forest rangers in the Jackson Hole where he spent the major part of his life.

He worked as a cattle drover, driving from the scuthwest to Canada, and in 1914 began working as a guide, a work for which he later became quite famed throughout the United States.

One of the great originals of the old West, Carrington was a man by himself. His colorful personality, marked by eccentricities made him an ideal subject for writers. Katherine Burt wrote a novel about him and Struthers Burt wrote an article, The Most Unforgettable Character I have Met for Readers Digest.

Carrington was considered one of the greatest guides and big game hunters in the West, a trait which helped considerably during a two year sting in Africa hunting big game.

Burial will be in the Jackson cemetery under the direction of the Rober Bean Funeral Home of Driggs.

26

Raised Eyebrows

On his deathbed, Cal had told Felicia he kept fifty dollars stashed in his boot and directed her to retrieve it from his cabin when he was gone. Sometime afterward, Felicia and her friend, Pearl Johnson, searched the cabin. They found the boot and the hidden fifty dollars. On a hunch there was more, Pearl told Felicia, "You don't know these oldtimers." More searching uncovered a cache where Cal had hidden a handgun, field glasses and a pair of brass knuckles. [1]

Cal bequeathed all his real and personal property to Felicia and Mary Frances Ake. His will probated and recorded in Driggs January 29, 1960, left all his real and personal property in Idaho to Felicia. [2] His will probated in San Diego on February 3, 1961, gave the money in his First National Bank of San Diego account to Felicia, but his real property in California was bequeathed to Mary Ake. Felicia later wrote that, "Mary Ake, a schoolteacher and Cal's childhood sweetheart, received half of Cal's estate."[3]

There must be a lot more to the Mary Ake story. In his will Cal referred to her as "an old pal since a kid." We know little about her or Cal's relationship with her. By the time of Cal's passing she was an old woman in poor health living in Mountain Home, Idaho. At times, in her later years, she may have also resided with her sister, Mrs. Paul Montgomery, in Seattle. Mary, also know as, "Mamie," was fourteen years younger than Cal.[4] In his 1958 interview, Cal said, "After I quit cowboying, I was down in Boise Valley country..." but did not elaborate further. Obviously, Mountain Home is a chapter in his life we know little about. In 1941, Cal spent part of the winter at Mountain Home, staying at the Hotel Mellen. He wrote, "My friends hear was all glad to see me, after [my] being gone nine years."[5]

Cal, true to himself to the end, however, did not give one-cent to his family, not even the customary one dollar.[6]

Who would believe an oldtime buckaroo would have had much more than his saddle or the old horse harnesses hung in his shack to leave to anyone? But when attorney Harold Forbush probated Cal's last will and testament, it was punctuated with a low whistle and eyebrows rose! While the origins of Cal's financial wealth may be attributable to Cissy in large part, Cal also had an uncanny aptitude for picking good investments. Moreover, he rarely spent any money on himself. In fact, he was more than frugal—at Bates he chose to live in relative destitution.

Attorney Forbush totaled it up: Cal had been receiving an annuity of one hundred dollars a month for life from the time he began working for Cissy, and he spent little of it. He had accounts in four different banks; a 23.72-acre tract and another lot next to Moonlight State Park in Encinitas, California; the 160-acre farm and cabin at Bates; stock in Greyhound Bus Lines, Coeur d'Alene mines and A.J. Industries; and his Willys Jeep.[7] The worth of his estate in terms of today's dollar was in the millions.

Felicia sold Cal's 160.29-acre Bates property to Oren Furniss—the neighbor boy Cal used to entertain with his stories—on January 18, 1962, for $21,000. And she eventually donated the black angora chaps Rose had, which Cal had long ago given to Cissy, to the Jackson Hole Historical Society and Museum. The chaps were displayed in a showcase at the Jackson play, *Petticoat Rules*, in 2001.

Years afterward, historian Wendell Gillette disclosed to former Jackson Museum Director Bob Rudd that he had visited Carrington's cabin right after his death and discovered an unlocked trunk in the cabin's attic containing personal belongings, including a matched pair of pistols laying side by side right on top. Gillette confided that he left the items where they were, but when he returned again to photograph the cabin, the trunk and its contents were gone.[8] Since Felicia didn't mention the trunk or its contents, it was previously assumed someone had absconded with it before she and Pearl Johnson had a chance to visit the cabin.

Gillette photographed Cal's cabin and remarked on its "sad condition." He recorded, "An old white suit hung in the closet, I bet it had made Cal look classy when in New York," but otherwise he noted, "There was very little left of an active cowboy's life."[9]

After whisperings circulated of Cal Carrington's financial worth, vandals repeatedly scoured his cabin, which stands alone in the center of the 160-acre parcel, hoping to find hidden money or valuables.[10] Rumors still persist that the old buckaroo had hidden money and valuables there.

Today, more than forty-five years after his death, the inside of Cal's stout old cabin has been trashed by the elements and looters. The old cookstove and harnesses shown in Gillette's 1959 photographs are gone, but the rough built bunk in the corner of the cabin, where the farm boys would sit to hear Cal's yarns, is still there; and the old wooden captain's chair, from which Cal once held court dispensing his stories, lies on its side next to the bunk.

Cal's friend Oren Furniss, in 2007 at age 89 on his horse, Chip.
Photo by the author.

27

Mysteries

Cal Carrington's earliest years in Jackson and elsewhere will always remain an incomplete and contradictory story, part of the myth and legends surrounding him and early-day Jackson Hole. Despite evidence to the contrary, some folks are understandably reluctant to give up on the cherished wild and woolly notion that he was an outlaw who hid stolen horses in Flat Creek Canyon. There's no question that's the way Cal would want it.

Cal is not recorded in early U.S. Census (the first he shows up is in 1930), nor in Social Security records. In contemporary language he was "off the grid." Combined with his use of multiple names, it does leave an impression that maybe he really was concealing something and hiding from his past. It's unlikely, however, but we'll probably never know for sure one way or the other. On the other hand, fiercely independent oldtimers often viewed those things as a government intrusion and avoided them. One thing for sure, though, Cal went out of his way not to mention anything about or related to his family to anyone.

When Cal finally does show up in a 1930 U.S. Census, it only raises more questions. How could he have been recorded at both Los Angeles and Cape Nome, Alaska? And what was he doing in Nome? Could this somehow have been a prank, more "playing with the truth" to confound us?

There is some evidence that, although he never married, Cal may have had children. Cissy's biographer Ralph Martin alludes to this, but doesn't tell all: "Before Cissy, women had been transients in his life. He had even refused to marry the woman who had borne his child,"[1] leaving one to wonder, who was she?

In correspondence with Felicia in the 1920s, Cissy jealously derided Cal for "having a baby" with Mary Ake.[2] Was this merely one of Cissy's "neat poisoned arrows shot into the air," or was it true? Could this have been the reason for Cal and Cissy's falling out around 1926? We can only speculate. Mary Ake's obituary makes no mention of any children.

Similarly, hand-written notes at the Jackson Hole Historical Society from Wendell Gillette's interview with Felicia contains mention of Cal having an affair with a Jackson married woman and a son born from that relationship. The notation indicates it may have been a woman from an esteemed family in Jackson's history.[3] A clue left for posterity perhaps, with no apparent way to connect it any longer to anything or anybody.

Who was Mary Frances Ake or "Mamie" as she was known by her family and friends? Social Security records and the recorded settlement of Cal's estate prove there was a Mary Ake who resided at Mountain Home, Idaho. She was the daughter of Frank and Laura Ake, a prominent Mountain Home pioneer family who were ranchers. Did Cal work on her father's ranch at one time? Was "Mary," in Cissy's novel *Glass Houses*, a composite of Mamie? Cissy wrote, "As soon as Mary was old enough to walk, she followed him [Cal] around her father's ranch."

Mary's obituary states she held a college degree from the University of Washington at Seattle and was a member of the Tri-Delta sorority. Obviously, it would seem she was more than just "an old pal" to Cal, since he bequeathed half of his estate to her.

Felicia wrote that Mamie was Cal's "childhood sweetheart" who had nursed him when he was sick and taught him to read and write. Still, records show she was fourteen years younger than Cal. She died in February 1967, at age seventy-six, and is buried at Mountain Home. It's curious that no correspondence has ever been uncovered between Cal and Mamie, since Cal generally kept the letters he received from friends. And it seems they would have corresponded, since he considered her an "old pal since childhood."

Cal carried on a long-distance relationship and correspondence with Goldie Chisman of San Diego for over thirty years. From later letters in the Felicia Gizycka Collection, it is apparent Goldie may have been a well-to-do business woman. She drove a Buick and helped Cal with real estate endeavors in southern California. But she was not above visiting Cal's cabin at Bates and wrote fondly of it. Record of their correspondence begins in 1928, after Cal returns from Africa, but it begs the question: how, when and where did they meet?

When Cal died, Felicia's friends helped find a stone that looked like the Grand Teton. Another friend in the East, a sculptor, made an impressive bronze plaque of a horse standing with an empty saddle, the reins dropped to the ground. Felicia phoned Rose Crabtree and told her about it. "You've done fine," Rose said, trying to conceal she was crying, "A ground-tied horse means a horse thief. And that's just what the old fool was."[4]

But today, Cal's grave is marked only by a small footstone simply reading: "Cal Carrington." What happened to the elaborate monument? Some still remember Cal's impressive marker in Aspen Cemetery. Jackson historian and *Teton Magazine* publisher Eugene Downer believes it was removed from the cemetery because it was feared someone would steal it. The plaque is among items being stored by the Jackson Hole Museum,[5] but no one seems to know where the rock monument to which it was once attached is located.

Flat Creek Ranch caretakers Forney Cole, Bob Stanton and another named Ritter always claimed the ranch was haunted. At times things would shake and rattle as if spirits possessed them. Stanton said, "There's ghosts...I saw and felt plenty." Ritter independently confirmed, "It sounded and felt as if all Hell had torn loose."[6] Today we know the ranch is located on a seismically active fault and occasional quakes rattle the property. It must have been terrifying for the caretakers who did not understand what was happening.

Still, rumors of the ranch being haunted persist. Recently, members of the Jackson Hole Land Trust swear they saw an aura in Cissy's restored cabin. Cal and Cissy were strong personalities; they will always haunt the Flat Creek Ranch and windswept precipices of Sheep Mountain.

Whatever became of the trapper's cabin in Flat Creek Canyon—where exactly was it located? No one remembers for sure. Charlie Peterson, Sr., recalled that "as you topped out, it sat on the left side of the road before you got to the other cabins." That is where present day ranch owner Joe Albright found the burned remnants.[7] The cabin where outlaws were rumored to have once hidden out has become a dim memory, a part of Jackson Hole's legends.

Finally, another puzzlement for people visiting the Flat Creek Ranch is the grand old piano in the lodge. Cissy had it taken into the ranch in 1929. It continues to mystify people how a wagon crew (actually with an ox cart) ever accomplished moving it to the ranch in one piece.

In the end, chronicling Cal's life history was an endeavor similar to putting together an old jigsaw puzzle where many of the pieces have been lost over time, and other pieces that somehow got into the box may not really belong there at all.

28
Legacy

Cal Carrington left a legacy of stories, handed down through literature and oral tradition, that richly figure in the mythos and legends surrounding Jackson Hole and the West.

Today Cal's Encinitas property is part of Village Park West, a residential subdivision. Only three and a half acres of his original 24.72-acre tract remain undeveloped, set aside for open space. The main street in the subdivision is named "Recluse Lane," after a retiring old cowboy who once hung out there, perhaps? Felicia remarked, "Cal lived in squalor there, just as he had in Driggs."[1]

In summer 2004, the ground at Cal's old homestead in Bates was planted with barley. His rustic cabin, weathered by more than a century, sat forlorn and abandoned in the center of the grain field. After the grain crop was harvested, flocks of migrating sandhill cranes staged in the field about the old shack. A few of today's oldtimers in Teton Valley know this was Cal Carrington's homestead, but otherwise most people passing by it on the Bates road have no idea that the cabin is steeped in Western lore, nor that its original owner was a celebrated early day Jackson Hole figure.

The beautifully restored Flat Creek Guest Ranch is a monument to Cal Carrington and Cissy Patterson. Nearly a century later those legendary original owners still hold dominion over the ranch. The ranch enjoys an incomparable wilderness setting, little changed from the time of Cal and Cissy. It remains as Cissy described in a 1944 letter, "Never anywhere in my life have I seen anything lovelier."[2] It's a place where guests can learn about and experience Jackson Hole, both as it was in the past and also what it's become.

The ranch is listed on the National Register of Historic Places, ironically, not because of the history surrounding it, but for the type of log work found in the original structures. Regardless, whatever served to qualify the ranch for listing, history justifies it.

Cissy's great-grandchildren, through Felicia and Drew Pearson's marriage and their daughter Ellen's family, Drew and Joe Arnold and their families at Laramie, Wyoming, went on to close a circle by becoming modern-day Jackson Hole skiers and skilled mountain climbers, creating a climbing and backpacking school they call Solid Rock. Joe Arnold is also an artist specializing in *plein air* mountainscapes. The Arnolds have a continuing attachment to Jackson Hole through a property at Turpin Meadows near Moran which Felicia assisted them in purchasing.

Joe Albright, Cissy's grandnephew, became the owner of the Flat Creek Ranch in 1996. A Conservation Easement donated by Josephine Patterson Reeve, and held by the Jackson Hole Land Trust, protects the property. The Cissy Patterson Trust supports its stewardship, in part. The canyon hideaway where legend has it that stolen horses were once hidden, where a spirited red-headed Countess found solace, and where an orphaned cowboy's life took an astonishing turn, is today preserved in perpetuity.

It is fitting that Cal's final resting place overlooks much more than the changed town of Jackson. The sweeping view up the valley takes in the open grasslands on the Elk Refuge, where Cal lived with Dick Turpin and John Holland when he first came to Jackson, and north to Miller's Butte, Flat Creek Canyon, Sheep Mountain, and the Tetons—all storied Jackson Hole places and ground intimately familiar to Cal. Thanks to conservation-minded individuals, its view still looks much the same today as when Cal first rode into the Hole more than a hundred years ago.

good luck

Cal

End Notes

Prologue

1 Mike Hurwitz, Western songwriter, Alta, WY, 2005.

2 Cissy Patterson was present-day ranch owner Joe Albright's grandaunt.

3 Burt, S. "The Most Unforgettable Character I've Met." *The Reader's Digest* (Oct 1948): 84.

Chapter 1

1 International Geneological Index.; Kathy Hodges, Research Specialist, Idaho Historical Society, Boise; and U.S. Census Records, Ancestry.com. Also it's reasonably certain that Cal knew and remembered his Swedish

shoemaker family origins as is evidenced in Felicia Gizycka's 1965 *Reminiscence* story in *Teton Magazine*. Cal's WWI draft card gives his birth date as February 10, 1875, but this may be another example of his practice of playing loose with the facts when responding to government questionnaires.

2 Forbush, H. *Tales of the Big Hole Mountains.* Idaho Falls, Idaho,(2000): 115-16 makes the connection to Albert Carrington, the prominent LDS leader. The website http://www.media.utah.edu/UHE/c/CARRINGTON, ALBERT.html describes Carrington as one of the intellectual leaders in the Mormon movement, who had a distinguished career involving the provisional government of Utah, territorial attorney general, presiding authority of the European Mission, one of the Twelve Apostles, president of the Perpetual Emigrating Fund Company, Church historian, and counselor to Brigham Young. He was also a polygamist with many wives and was excommunicated from the church in the later part of his life "for crimes of lewd and lascivious conduct and adultery." Some sources give Cal's age as five-years old when he was taken by the missionaries.

3 Gizycka, F. "Jackson Hole, 1916-65: A Reminiscence." *Vogue*, (April 1, 1965): 200-03. A February 19, 1960, Earl and Sadie Harris letter in the Felicia Gizycka Collection (courtesy of Amanda Smith) states that a four-year-old brother was also taken by the Missionaries and accompanied Enoch to the U.S. They were apparently split up upon their arrival in Utah. Enoch's brother was adopted by a family named Price, but died at the age of six. He is reportedly buried under the name of Julin in the Salt Lake Cemetery. Felicia Gizycka, although she was aware of

this, does not mention Cal's younger brother in the *Vogue* or other articles she later writes about Cal (see 2/19/60 Earl and Sadie Harris letter in the Felecia Gizycka Collection). I have kept the story as originally told by others, without introducing the fact Cal's younger brother appears to have traveled with him to Utah.

4 Gizycka, F. "Cissy Patterson: The Countess of Flat Creek." *Teton Magazine*, Vol. 10 (1977): 37-48. Also: Utah death records show Gustaf died of chronic Brights disease April 7, 1917; Julia of intestinal parasites June 23, 1919. Both are buried in the Salt Lake City cemetery. Cal's brother, Zeneiph, actually appears to have tried to connect with him in Driggs as early as 1946 (see Felicia Gizycka Collection).

5 U.S. Census Records/Ancestry.com

6 At that time steamboats traveled from Liverpool to New York. In 2004 port of entry records were searched for a Carrington or Julin around the dates he could have arrived, but without success.

7 Gizycka, F. *A Reminiscence*, 1965. Cal told Cissy his mother had sold him to a captain of a sailing ship in England. The use of the word "sailing" may have been used more broadly and may not necessarily mean a ship with sails, per se.

8 Forbush, H. Pers. Comm. w/author, 2004.

9 Declaration of Intention to Become a Citizen of the United States, National Archives and Teton County Idaho Court House records, 1901. An April 12, 1961, letter to Felicia Gizycka by Enoch's brother Zeneiph J. Julin in the Felicia Gizycka Collection states, "Cal purposely misrepresented his nationality and birthplace and would not acknowledge otherwise."

10 Burt, S. *The Diary of a Dude Wrangler*. Charles Scribner's Sons, (1901): 306; also in: Healy, P.F. *Cissy: A Biography of Eleanor M. "Cissy" Patterson*. 1966.

11 Gizycka, F. *A Reminiscence*. 1965. There is conflicting evidence whether Cal's growing up with his foster family was entirely within Utah, or whether the foster family at some point moved to the Boise Valley. In either case, Cal spent some time at Mountain Home in his early years. Burt, S. *The Most Unforgettable Character...* states, "at age eight Cal was adopted by a couple with a ranch in Idaho." Forbush's notes state Cal's foster family was at Logan. A handwritten note on a Jackson Lodge No. 1713 envelope by Felicia in December 1959 says he "went to [a] community called Smithfield." This is a small town north of Logan, which is further substantiated by Forbush's general location of Logan.

12 University of Wyoming 1957 recorded interview. Transcribed by Bonney and Bonney. From the personal files of Loraine Bonney, Kelly, WY.

13 Stone, D. Recorded Oral Interview, Teton County Idaho Historical Society, 1958. Arranged by Harold Forbush. Tape is on file at the Historical Society in Driggs.

14 Cal told this to the Harris' when he was staying at their Driggs motel near the end of his life, they passed it along to Felicia; see: Gizycka, *A Reminiscence*. 1965. Burt also recorded it in *The Most Unforgettable Character...*

15 Alluded to and mentioned in several sources.

16 University of Wyoming 1957 recorded interview conducted by Cliff Hansen and faculty at Laramie, WY. (from a transcription in the personal files of Lorraine Bonney, Kelly, WY.)

Chapter 2

1 University of Wyoming. Cal Carrington oral interview transcribed by Bonney and Bonney, 1957. (From the personal files of Lorraine Bonney, Kelly, WY.)

2 Burt, S. "The Most Unforgettable Character I've Met." *Reader's Digest* (Oct 1948): 83-86. Carrington does not use the name Cal in his signature on early documents. He signs as Enoch Carrington. The author speculates he was dubbed "California" or "Cal" when he returned to Jackson Hole after having worked in California for two years; or perhaps it's then Cal thought to apply the name to himself. But his taking the name "California, after a cowboy he admired" is a more interesting and long-standing story. The name Carrington may have been applied to him by the Port of Immigration Authority in New York when he first entered the country, especially if he was in fact traveling in the company of Albert Carrington.

3 Ibid. Burt has Cal cowboying for about twenty years, but this doesn't necessarily mesh with Cal's date of arrival in Teton Basin and what is known about his other activities. His early years as a drover, saddle tramp and bronc rider appear to have been more like eight years versus the twenty attributed by Burt.

4 Stone, D. Recorded oral interview with Cal Carrington. Teton Valley Historical Society, Driggs, ID, 1958. Also transcribed and on file at JHHSM, Jackson, WY. In the Dwight Stone 1958 interview in Driggs, Cal, for whatever reason, refused to talk about his early cowboy days or where he had been before coming into the Tetons, telling the interviewer, "That's none of your damn business," or "Let's not talk about

that." The U. of Wyoming interview provides information on years that previously were pretty much a mystery or question as to Cal's whereabouts and activities. Of course, there is always the issue of whether Cal's stories were true happenings and how much was simply passed around cowboy lore.

5 University of Wyoming interview, 1957, op.cit. The correct spelling might be Twodot versus Todot?

6 Ibid. Also in *Glass Houses*, Cissy fictionalized a take on this story where she had Cal involved in driving 500 head of stolen cattle from the Southwest up into the north.

7 Ibid.

8 This remark by Cal in the U. of Wyoming interview in reference to some of his wilder cowboy years contradicts those who like to believe he was an outlaw in those times.

9 University of Wyoming interview, 1957, op.cit.

10 Ibid.

Chapter 3

1 Healy, P.F. *Cissy: A Biography of Eleanor M. "Cissy" Patterson*. Doubleday 1966.

2 Burt, S. *The Diary of a Dude Wrangler*. Charles Scribner's Sons, NY, 1924.

3 Burt, N. *Jackson Hole Journal*. University of Oklahoma Press, 1983.

4 Burt, S. *The Most Unforgettable Character...* 1948, op.cit.

5 Martin, R.G. *The Extraodinary Life of Eleanor Medill Patterson*. Simon and Shuster, NY.

6 Burt, N. *Jackson Hole Journal...* 1983, op.cit.

7 Burt, S. *Diary...* 1948, op. cit. Burt says, Cal taught himself to read and write at age twenty-one.

8 His friend Felicia Gizycka stated he learned to read and write from Mary Ake in *Teton Magazine*, Vol. 10, 1948. While Felicia stated Cal "was barely literate," this is a relative judgment. Felicia was well educated and a writer. For the place and time and comparing him to many contemporaries, he was not illiterate. The author has seen a good number of letters written by him, which demonstrated his capability to read, write and carry on a correspondence (see the Felicia Gizycka Collection). Spelling was not his forté. Cal's literacy is not accurately represented by his 1952 typewritten letter to Josephine Albright alone. Early archival documents bear Cal's well-practiced "Enoch Carrington" signature, but in later personal correspondence, he'd simply sign as "Cal" with an artful flourish.

9 Forbush, H. Pers. Comm. 2004.

10 Burt, N. *Jackson Hole Journal...* 1979, op.cit.

11 Gillette, B. *Homesteading with the Elk.* Jackson Printing, 1992. As a woman, Bertha would have witnessed Cal's cowboy gallantry when he would stop off at their homestead to visit.

12 Hoge, A.A. *Cissy Patterson: The Life of Eleanor Medill Patterson Publisher and Editor of the Washington Times-Herald.* Random House, NY, 1966.

13 University of Wyoming 1957 oral interview transcription by Bonney and Bonney.

14 Stone, D. Recorded oral interview, 1958. op. cit.

Chapter 4

1 Gillette, W. "The Memorable Character – Cal Carrington. *Snake River Echoes." A Quarterly of Idaho History.* Teton Co. Ed., Vol.8, No. 3. 54-62. A water right filing by Cal in April 1897, on record in the Teton County, Idaho, courthouse substantiates this arrival date for Teton Valley. Teton Valley was known to the mountain men and early explorers as Pierre's Hole; Mormon settlers called it Teton Basin; today it's known as Teton Valley.

2 Ibid.

3 Stone, D. Recorded oral interview with Cal Carrington. Teton Valley Historical Society, Driggs, 1958. Some have suspiciously viewed Cal and Berger's arrival in Teton Valley together, trying to link the two men as partners engaged in rustling. All evidence is to the contrary. Both men were looking for land to homestead in Teton Valley. Both men took up land. Berger settled down, married, raised a family, and was later recognized as being among early upstanding Mormon pioneers in the Victor area. He is buried in the Victor cemetery.

4 Stone, D. Oral interview, 1958. op.cit.

5 Gillette, W. *The Memorable Character...* 1979. op.cit.

6 Stone, D. Oral interview, 1958, op.cit.

7 *The Desert News* quoted in Moss, W. "The Avenues of Driggs Tell a Story." *Teton Valley Top to Bottom.* (Summer 2006): 50-55.

8 Owen, W. 1892. Bill Barlow's Budget, 9 June 1886. Reprinted in *JHHSM Chronicle* Fall 2006.

9 Thompson, Edith M.S. and William Leigh Thompson. *Beaver Dick: The Honor and the Heartbreak.* Jelm Mt. Press, Laramie, 1982.

10 *Teton Valley News* quoted in Moss, W. *The Avenues of Driggs...* 2006. op.cit.

11 Gillette, W. *The Memorable Character...* 1979; and also, Stone, D. Oral Interview, 1958.

12 BLM GLO National Archives (accessed through: http://www.glorecords.blm.gov/) Berger went the Homestead Act route, while Cal made entry under the Desert Land Act.

13 Driggs, B.W. *History of Teton Valley.* Arnold Agency, Rexburg, ID, 1970.

14 Stone, D. Oral interview, 1958. op.cit. Interestingly, Langford with the 1872 Hayden Party made a similar observation about Teton Valley's prairies, remarking that they were "carpeted with the heaviest and largest bunchgrass" he had ever seen.

Chapter 5

1 Driggs, B.W. *History of Teton Valley.* Arnold Agency, Rexburg, ID, 1970 ed.

2 Land and patent records, Teton County, Idaho, courthouse. The records at Blackfoot and Oasis were later moved to Driggs after Teton County, Idaho, was created.

3 National Archives, BLM-GLO, Desert Land case no. 3116.

4 Land and patent records, Teton County, Idaho courthouse; also National Archives. Cal purposely misrepresented his country of origin.

5 National Archives, op.cit.

6 Ibid.

7 Gillette, W. *The Memorable Character...* 1979, op.cit.

8 Stone, D. 1958, op.cit.; also, O.H. Bonney and L.G. Bonney. *Bonney's Guide: Grand Teton National Park and Jackson Hole.* Houston, TX, (Trip 12, 1972): 122-23. Bonney and Bonney refer to Cal as "a crony" of John Holland; evidence indicates they were good friends.

9 The BLM states, "95% of the early Desert Land Act claims were bogus" (see website: http://www.reference.com/browse/wiki/Desert-Land Act)

10 National Archives case no. 3116, op.cit.

11 Ibid.

12 Ibid.

13 Platts, D. 1991. *John Cherry: His Lies, Life and Legend.* Bearpaw Press, Jackson, WY.

14 It's doubtful that Cal spent many winters at Bates or in Jackson Hole in the early years. More likely he rode south into warmer climes or over to the Boise valley, where the author speculates he may have worked sometime or another at the Frank Ake Ranch in Mountain Home. At times he may have also boarded the train at Rexburg or St. Anthony and ridden south, returning to Bates in spring to work on his desert entry claim, after which he'd go over to Jackson Hole for seasonal ranch work and wrangling and packing for Yellowstone Park or the Forest Service. He was a man on the move.

Chapter 6

1 Stone, D. Recorded oral interview, 1958; also in Gillette, W. *The Memorable Character...* 1979.

2 Ibid. Cal used this line frequently in his later years in response to questions he didn't want to answer directly. It was recorded by several authors and also in his 1957 University of Wyoming interview. Interestingly, he doesn't use the complete saying, which was generally spoken as, "...didn't have nothing but a long rope and a running iron."

3 Holmes, B.M. *Victor, Idaho, 1889-1989.* Mimeo (on file at the Valley of the Tetons Library, Victor, Idaho) 1989.

4 Daugherty, J. *A Place Called Jackson Hole.* National Park Service, Moose, (1999): 180-82.

5 Wards hotel and store (see Daugherty, J. *A Place Called Jackson Hole,* (1999): 209.)

6 Daugherty, J. 1999, op.cit.

7 Wilson, C. *The Return of the White Indian.* Fenske Printing, Inc., Rapid City, SD (1985): 151-375. Charles Wilson provides a detailed account of the dangers and difficulties of early day crossing of the Snake River at Wilson.

8 Ibid

9 University of Wyoming interview, 1957.

10 Bonney, O.H. and L.G. Bonney. *Bonney's Guide: Grand Teton national Park and Jackson's Hole.* Houston, TX, (Trip 13, 1972): 122-23. (The material the Bonney's cite came from Cal's 1957 University of Wyoming interview).

11 Anyone who came into the Hole before 1915 was

considered an oldtimer. See Charles Wilson. *Return of the White Indian,* 1985, op.cit.

12 University of Wyoming, Recorded oral interview, 1957; also in Bonney and Bonney, 1972. Cal claimed Holland let Dick Turpin off because he was a member of the Jackson Hole brotherhood.

13 University of Wyoming interview, 1957.

14 Platts, D. *Robert Miller: An Enigma.* Wilson, WY, 2003. A newspaper story that Platts uncovered quotes outlaw Teton Jackson as saying, "Miller and Holland were providing him and his men supplies." Similar undocumented allegations are mentioned in other sources as well.

15 Gillette, W. "The Memorable Character—Cal Carrington." *A Quarterly of Idaho History. Snake River Echoes,* Teton County, Idaho, (Vol. 8, No. 3. 1979)

16 Dyke, J.C. *The West of the Texas Kid, 1881-1910: Recollections of Thomas E. Crawford.* Norman Univ. of Oklahoma Press, 1962.

17 Betts, R.B. *Along the Ramparts of the Tetons.* Colorado Assoc. Univ. Press, Boulder, 1978.

18 University of Wyoming interview, 1957.

19 Stone, D. Recorded oral interview, 1958.

20 Brown, D. *Wondrous Times on the Frontier.* August House Publishers. Little Rock, 1991. Brown describes and analyzes the Westerners' practice of "stringing greeners." Like Cal, Cissy was very adept at creating and modifying stories and substituting or putting Cal into those tales, see *Glass Houses.*

21 Burt, N. Jackson Hole Journal... 1983, op.cit.

22 Peterson, C. Oral interviews by the author, 2004/2005.

23 Gizycka, F. "Jackson Hole, 1916-65: A Reminiscence." *Vogue* (April 1, 1965): 209.

24 Martin, Hoge and Healy all give these stories about Cal in their biographies on Cissy. These tales appear to have been taken from Cissy's novel, *Glass Houses*, pp200-201. They undoubtedly originated from Cal's yarns, but were embellished or modified to fit her story line. For example, in his 1957 interview, Cal told a story about Ed Hunter, who was arrested and brought in for poaching. The lawmen, as Cal told it, took Hunter into a saloon with them, and while they were having a drink, Hunter walked out the back door and lit out, swam the river and escaped. The lawmen declined to cross the river after him. In *Glass Houses*, Cissy writes it was Cal (Ben) who escaped the posse by swimming the river. This appears to be the source of the story of Cal swimming the ice-swollen Snake River to escape a posse that was later picked up and passed along by journalists as fact.

25 University of Wyoming recorded oral interview, 1957.

26 Ibid.

27 Burt, Struthers. *The Most Unforgetable Character I've Met.* 1948, op.cit.

28 Burt, S. *The Diary of a Dude Wrangler.* Charles Scribner's Sons, (1924): 305.

29 Huyler, J. *And That's the Way it Was in Jackson Hole.* Jackson Hole Hist. Soc. & Museum, 2003. Playing with names was a common practice in those days. Changing

one's name might mean there was something to hide, but on the other hand, for example, Cissy was known by multiple names too: Cissy Patterson, Eleanor Patterson, Eleanor Medill Gizycka, Countess Eleanor, the Countess, the Countess of Flat Creek, etc.

30 Gillette, W. *The Memorable Character...* 1979; see also the Flat Creek Ranch's history website.

31 Healy, P.F. *Cissy: A Biography of Eleanor M. "Cissy" Patterson.* Doubleday, 1966.

32 Gillette, W. *The Memorable Character...* 1979. It's interesting that Gillette, who was a local historian, would not catch the inconsistencies in the dates of Cal's alleged "horse thieving ring," especially in respect to the 1920s date when Cal actually took up squatters rights on the Flat Creek Ranch. Gillette claimed, "All the rustlers were caught except Cal," but there is no record of anyone ever being apprehended for rustling around that time. This was also a story Rose Crabtree told about Cal before Gillette picked it up. It's repeated in, Adare, S. *Jackson Hole Uncovered*, et al., 1997; and the Flat Creek Ranch website.

33 Martin, R.G. 1979; also in Gillette, 1979; and the Flat Creek Ranch website.

34 Platts, D. *The Cunningham Ranch Incident.* Wilson, WY, 1992; also in Betts, R.B. *Along the Ramparts...* 1978; and, Anderson, M. "Last of Jackson's Hole Horse Thieves." *The Westerner* (Aug. 24, 1929). Anderson states, as this author also concludes after research, that the last days of any organized or significant horse rustling in and around Jackson Hole occurred in the early 1890s. The 1892 Cunningham Cabin incident appears to have marked the end of it.

35 The Flat Creek Ranch website, Rose Crabtree, et.al., claim Cal belonged to these "gangs" and that they were a part of organized rustling in the Jackson Hole area in the early twentieth century. In actuality, as explained in Chapter 7, these cliques existed for other purposes or reasons and were mostly before Cal's time in Jackson Hole. Yet they are frequently recalled in myths about Cal's horse rustling, e.g.: "Cal belonged to a gang of six [rustlers] identified by the red bandanas they wore, all the outlaws were captured except Cal."

Chapter 7

1 Moss, W. "Friend or Faux." *Teton Valley Top to Bottom.* (Summer 2003): 62-67. See also: C. Wilson. *The Return of the White Indian,* 1985.

2 Ibid.

3 Dyke, J. *The West Texas Kid, 1881-1910: Recollections of Thomas E. Crawford.* Univ. Oklahoma Press, 1962.

4 Platts, D. John Cherry: *His Lies, Life and Legend.* Bearprint Press, Jackson, WY 1991.

5 Ibid.

6 Brandegee, T.S. *Annual Rept. U.S. Geol. Survey, 1878-98 of the Teton Forest Reserve.* General Land Office, Washington, D.C.

7 University of Wyoming interview, 1957.

8 Martin, R.G. *Cissy: The Extraordinary Life of Eleanor Medill Patterson.* Simon and Schuster. NY, 1979. See also Flat Creek Ranch history website.

9 Bonney, O.H. and L.G. Bonney. *Grand Teton National Park and Jackson's Hole*. Houston, Texas, (Trip 12, 1972): 122-23.

10 Calkins, F. *Jackson Hole*. Alfred A. Knopf, NY, 1973.

11 Ibid.

12 Ibid. One wonders where John Carnes was that winter since sources say he settled in Jackson Hole in 1884.

13 Platts, D. *Robert Miller: An Enigma*. Wilson, WY, 2003. (see letter quoting Teton Jackson re. supplies).

14 An old photograph (c 1908-1909) of Cal as a young man posing with four other men (one is John Holland) is sometimes pointed to as part of the gang of six. However, Felicia Gizycka in a *Teton Magazine* article identifies the photograph as being an antelope hunting party. No doubt it's the same early antelope hunting trip Struthers Burt writes about in *Diary of a Dude Wrangler* and Cal also talks about in his 1957 interview.

15 Driggs, B.W. *History of Teton Valley, Idaho*, 1970.

16 Wister, O. *The Virginian*. Macmillan Co., 1902.

17 Platts, D. *The Cunningham Ranch Incident*. Self published. Wilson, WY, 1992.

18 Driggs, B.W. *History of Teton Valley, Idaho*, 1970.

19 USF&WS Natl Elk Refuge, *Timeline of the Miller Ranch and National Elk Refuge History* pamphlet.

20 Platts, *Cunningham Ranch Incident*; Betts, *Along the Ramparts...*; also Mumey, N. *The Teton Mountains: Their History and Tradition*; et al.

21 Wilson, C. *The Return of the White Indian*, 1985, op.cit..

22 In Platts, D. *The Cunningham Ranch Incident*, 1992, op.cit.

23 Bonney, O.H. and L.G. Bonney. *Bonney's Guide: Grand Teton National Park and Jackson's Hole*. Houston, TX, (Trip 12, 1972): 122-23.

24 Stone, D. Recorded oral interview, 1958.

25 See D. Platts, *The Cunningham Ranch Incident and Robert Miller, An Enigma*; R. Betts, *Along the Ramparts of the Tetons*; F. Caulkins, *Jackson Hole*; B.W. Driggs, *History of Teton Valley*; C Wilson, *Return of the White Indian*; M. Anderson, *Last of Jackson's Hole Horse Thieves*. These authors, and this author as well, searched primary sources for any organized rustling incidents in and around Jackson Hole after the early 1890s, there are none recorded. *Helena's Daily Independent* reported on and sensationalized the rustling events that occurred in the early 1890s. Montana rancher John Chapman was one of the hired regulators. He had a personal axe to grind, after having lost a large number of valuable horses and tracking them to Jackson Hole. The regulators with the unknowing local posse at Cunningham Cabin; George Parker's (aka Butch Cassidy) capture at Star Valley; Sylvester Summers capture at Wolverine, Idaho; and Jack Bliss and Kid Collier's demise at the hands of range detectives all occurred around this time as a result of a Montana stock grower's organized dragnet.

Chapter 8

1 University of Wyoming recorded oral interview, 1957. Undated transcription by Bonney and Bonney obtained from the personal files of Loraine Bonney.

2 National Archives, GLO Special Agent Brighton's 1907 letter.

3 University of Wyoming, recorded oral interview proceedings personally described to the author by G.M. Gressley, retired history professor, in 2007. The Dwight Stone interview was conducted at Driggs a year later.

4 University of Wyoming, 1957, recorded oral interview. Undated transcription by Bonney and Bonney obtained from the personal files of Loraine Bonney. The YNP surveys in the Lamar that might have been going on at that time were suggested by historian Lee H. Whittlesey in a 2007 phone conversation.

5 Ibid.

6 Ibid. Leigh died in 1899; while it's possible that Cal could have met him on the trail a year before his death, it's more likely this is one of Cal's entertaining fabrications.

7 Ibid.

8 Ibid.

9 Anderson, A.A. *Experiences and Impressions: The Autobiography of Colonel A.A. Anderson.* McMillan Company, NY, (1933): 89-116. The survey of Forest Reserve corresponds with the date when Cal was hired by Anderson. The survey required a number of wranglers and large numbers of pack stock.

10 University of Wyoming interview, 1957, op.cit. John Holland is generally said to have sold his Nowlin Creek homestead and left Jackson in 1900, but he already had a Desert Entry Patent on 160 acres on Horseshoe Creek in Teton Valley in 1989 and followed up with an adjacent

160-acre homestead purchase there in 1900 (GLO records). He remained in the Teton Valley-Jackson Hole area for another 6-7 years.

11 Ibid.

12 Ibid.

13 Daugherty, J. et.al. *A Place Called Jackson Hole. Grand Teton National Park*, Moose, WY, (1999): 295.

14 University of Wyoming interview, op.cit.

15 Ibid. A.A. Anderson also describes this incident and gives the name of the sheepman as Jacob.

16 Anderson, A.A., op.cit.

17 Ibid.

18 University of Wyoming interview, op.cit.; also A.A. Anderson, op.cit.

19 National archives and Teton Valley, Idaho, courthouse records, Sworn Declaration of Intention. Although Cal's naturalization certification cites England as his birthplace or place of origin, evidence shows he was born in Sweden and immigrated to the United States through England (see Chapter 1). There have been numerous instances giving his birthplace as England, or even Norway (e.g., see the Flat Creek Ranch website). Cal purposely misrepresented his birthplace because of the bad feelings he harbored towards his family.

20 National Archives, Enoch Carrington's 1905 USDA Forest Service Certificate of Appointment as Assistant Forest Ranger.

21 Layser, E.F. "Lone Rangers." *Teton Valley Top to Bottom.* (Winter, 2001): 52-57.

22 Marsh, S. "Abandoned Trails" in *Stories of the Wild*, White Willow Publishing, Jackson, WY (2001): 237-243.

23 Martin, R.G. 1979, op.cit.

24 Daugherty, J. 1999, op.cit.

25 Anderson, A.A. 1933, op.cit.

26 National Archives. Patent approval letter by authority of Theodore Roosevelt, 1907.

27 Cissy's biographers Martin, R.G. and Hoge, A.A. both say Cal was in San Francisco during the 1906 earthquake.

28 National Archives, GLO July 22, 1907 report by Inspector Brighton, Salt Lake City, Utah.

29 University of Wyoming interview, op.cit. It's speculation, but Cal may have been stationed on the Plumas National Forest at Quincy. He named a pack mare Quincy, the one that supposedly, as he told Felicia, "came along in the dark of the night."

30 Martin, R.G. 1979, p157.

31 Approval of Cal's Bates Desert Entry and his return from California coincide in respect to the date.

Chapter 9

1 Smith, B., E. Cole and D. Dobkin. *Imperfect Pasture*. USF&WS and Teton Nat. History Assoc., Jackson, 2004.

2 Thompson, E.M.S. and W.L. Thompson. *Beaver Dick: The Honor and the Heartbreak*. Jelm Mt. Press, Laramie, 1982.

3 Calkins, F. *Jackson Hole*. Alfred A. Knopf, NY, 1973.

4 University of Wyoming interview, 1957.

5 Daugherty, J. *A Place Called Jackson Hole.* National Park Service, Moose, 1999.

6 Mumey, N. *The Teton Mountains: Their History and Tradition.* 1948, op.cit.

7 *Jackson Hole Courier.*

8 Daugherty, J. *A Place Called Jackson Hole.* 1999, op cit.

9 Ibid, 139.

10 University of Wyoming interview, 1957.

11 Daugherty, J. 1999, op.cit.

12 Ibid.

13 National Archives, Affidavit of Witness, June 5, 1901.

14 University of Wyoming 1957 interview.

15 Ibid. While it is generally thought that Holland moved to "Salem," this could not be verified. An obituary could not be found in the Portland, Salem or Roseburg newspapers for Holland. He apparently located somewhere in the general area of those three places.

16 John Carnes Obituary, July 16, 1931. Owen Collection (Lorraine Bonney files, Kelly, Wy).

17 Bonney and Bonney, op. cit., 122-23.

18 Ibid.

19 Peterson, C. Sr. Pers. comm. w/author, 2005.

20 Last of the old West interview series taped by Jo Ann Byrd, JHHSM. Jackson. Jay Lawson in *Men to Match our Mountains* (p100) says Billy Bierer and Albert Nelson built a Flat Creek cabin in 1894 when they were trapping the

Jackson Hole country. This is consistent with Charlie Peterson also attributing the cabin to Bierer. Whether or not this is the same cabin Cal used isn't totally certain, but appears likely.

21 A number of authors have passed along the myth that Flat Creek Canyon was used by Cal to hide stolen horses; while presumably, Cal and his outlaw associates lived in the cabin. These included Martin, Healy, Gillette, and others.

22 Gizycka, F. "Forgiveness at Flat Creek." Teton Magazine, (Vol. 20, 1988): 27. The pack mare named Quincy may have in actuality been named after the town or area where Cal was stationed when he worked for the Forest Service in California. While this is a good story, it's not likely Quincy was actually stolen by Cal.

23 Stone, D. Recorded oral interview, 1958; and also, University of Wyoming interview, 1957.

24 Thompson, G. Pers. comm. w/author, 2004.

25 Furniss, O. Pers. comm. w/author, 2004.

26 Daugherty, J. (1999): 192, op.cit.

27 The closest law officer was at Evanston in those days, which tended to encourage Jackson Holers to take care of any problems themselves. The local brand of justice was called "mountain law."

28 Platts, D. *John Cherry: His Lies, Life and Legend.* Bearprint Press, Jackson, 1991.

Chapter 10

1 University of Wyoming recorded oral interview, 1957.

2 Ibid.

3 Ibid.

4 Ibid.

5 Ibid.

6 Bonney and Bonney 1972, op.cit.

7 Gillette, W. *The Memorable Character,* 1979, op.cit.

8 University of Wyoming interview, 1957.

9 Dwight Stone recorded interview, 1958. Teton Valley Historical Society.

10 McBride, M. *My Diary.* Unpublished mimeo. Jackson Hole Historical Society files, 1896.

11 University of Wyoming recorded interview, 1957.

12 Moss, W.F. "Those Were The Days My Friend." *Teton Valley Top to Bottom.* (Winter 2005): 56-61.

13 University of Wyoming recorded interview, 1957.

14 Buchan, D. "Ties to the Past." *Teton Valley Magazine.* (Winter 2007-08): 74-83; and, Pers. Comm. w/Clifford Hansen, 2008.

15 Burt, S. "The Most Unforgettable Character I've Met." *Reader's Digest.* (Oct 1948): 83-86.

16 Burt, S. *The Diary of a Dude Wrangler,* 1924, op.cit.

Chapter 11

1 Daugherty, J. *A Place Called Jackson Hole...*(1999): 225, op.cit.

2 University of Wyoming interview, 1957.

3 Burt, S. *The Most Unforgettable Character...* 1948, op.cit; Gizycka, F. "Forgiveness at Flat Creek." *Teton Magazine.* (Vol. 20, 1988): 8-9, 26-32.

4 Cal is frequently credited with having made this statement, implying that he had retired from being an outlaw, but in fact he had already been guiding dudes with John Holland for a number of years before he went to work for Burt and was already, at the time, working for Burt as ranch foremen.

5 University of Wyoming interview, 1957.

6 Burt, N. *Jackson Hole Journal.* University of Oklahoma Press, 1983.

7 Burt, S. *The Most Unforgettable Character...* 1948, op.cit.

8 Burt, N. 1983. *Jackson Hole Journal.* op.cit. In *Glass Houses* (p262), Cissy states you could hear everyone snore through the hotel's "flimsy room partitions."

9 Interview with Hank Crabtree, Ralph Martin collection, Boston University, Howard Gotlieb Archival Center (Box 213,F4).

10 Jackson Hole newspaper articles on Fourth of July rodeo entries were searched around this time period, but none listed Carrington, perhaps indicating by that time he had given up on rodeo and bronc riding.

11 Burt, N. 1983, op.cit.

Chapter 12

1 Gizycka, F. "Cissy Patterson: The Countess of Flat Creek." *Teton Magazine*. (Vol.10, 1977): 37-48.

2 Holmes, B. M. *Victor, Idaho, 1889-1989*. Bound mimeo. Valley of the Tetons Library, 1989.

3 Gizycka, F. *Cissy...* (1977): 39, op.cit.

4 Burt, N. *Jackson Hole Journal*. University of Oklahoma Press, 1983.

5 Gizycka, F. *Cissy...* 1977, op.cit.

6 Ibid.

7 Ibid, 40.

8 Martin, R.G. "Letters to Rose." Also *Teton Magazine*. (Vol. 12, 1979): 8-11, 27-28, 44-62.

9 Gizycka, F. *Cissy...* 1977, op.cit.

10 Ibid.

11 Gizycka, F. "Forgiveness at Flat Creek." *Teton Magazine*, (Vol. 20, 1988): 27.

12 A question about Cal and Cissy's relationship that was frequently asked the author, "was it ever consummated?" The only doubt comes from Felicia's spin in later years. For whatever reason she claimed: "They loved each other, but not in that way...Cal was too dirty and smelly." Hardly. Both Cal and Cissy were very physical and attractive people. Cissy possessed a sophisticated attitude about men and relationships;

Cal was considered a ladies' man. Cissy has been described by other writers as "the wildest woman in Jackson Hole," and Cal as a "wild man." They were one of the most celebrated "dude affairs" in Jackson Hole's history; another writer called it a "passionate love affair." Cissy sought out adventure and always had many suitors. Biographer Martin, said she tried to encourage Rose Crabtree to have an affair. Until their falling out and Cissy's marriage to Elmer Schlesinger in 1924, for about eight years, while on hunting trips, Cal and Cissy slept together in tents (Charlie Peterson in an interview said, "Cal drug his saddle in her tent and stayed"). They attended parties together, built the Flat Creek Ranch together, and traveled abroad together to events such as Josephine Baker performing in the nude in Paris. In *Glass Houses*, Cissy writes about the smell of "strong, healthy and unwashed men," indicating she did not find it offensive, but rather a matter-of-fact and exciting part of her Western experience. Readers should be able to pretty much make up their own minds on the question.

13 Martin, R.G. *Cissy: The Extraordinary Life of Eleanor Medill Patterson.* Simon and Schuster, NY, 1979. p 159.

14 Burt, N. *Jackson Hole Journal.* University of Oklahoma Press, 1983.

15 The "small secret valley..." quote is from Cissy's 1926 *Glass Houses*; "without psychiatry..." is taken from Gizycka, F. *Cissy...* 1977, op.cit.

16 Burt, S. *The Most Unforgettable Character...* 1948, op.cit.

17 Burt, S. *Jackson Hole Journal,* 1983, op.cit.

Chapter 13

1 Martin, R.G. *Cissy: The Extraordinary Life of Eleanor Mendill Peterson.* Simon and Schuster, NY, 1979. Cal's "reluctance "to sell is a story repeated often in the literature, but it appears that it is a myth created by Cal and Cissy themselves. Cissy's opinion of the Flat Creek Ranch's beauty never changed over the years. In a 1944 letter to Joseph Patterson, Cissy wrote, "Never in my life anywhere have I seen anything lovelier than this place..." (Patterson Papers, Lake Forest College, IL).

2 Martin, R.G. *Cissy: The Extraordinary Life...* 1979, op.cit.

3 Flat Creek Ranch website describes the process undertaken to prove up and Cal's "improvements" based on National Archive records.

4 The Jackson Hole Historical Society and Museum has Cal's artistically made branding iron, Object No. 1958.700.1. No brand is known to have been registered for the Flat Creek Ranch by Cissy.

5 Stone, D. Oral interview, 1958. Twenty-five head of livestock reported in the National Archive records is probably the truer number than Cal's fifty head mentioned in the interview.

6 Ryan, J. Pers. comm. w/author, 2004.

7 Gillette, B. *Homesteading with the Elk.* Jackson Printing, 1992.

8 Peterson, C. Sr. Pers. comm. w/author, 2004.

9 Gillette, B. *Homesteading...* 1992, op.cit.

10 December 27, 1922 Letter from Cal Carrington to Eleanor

Gizycka, Patterson Family Papers, Late Forest College, Il. (courtesy of Amanda Smith).

11 Thompson, G. Pers. comm. w/author, 2004.

12 Ibid.

Chapter 14

1 Martin, R.G. *Cissy: The Extraordinary Life of Eleanor Medill Patterson.* Simon and Schuster, NY, 1979. The remark is attributed to Joe Patterson (Patterson Papers, Lake Forest, IL).

2 The website www.culturaltourism.org/dch pictures and describes the mansion.

3 Martin, R.G. *Cissy...* 1979. This issue in Cissy and Cal's relationship appears to have been overstated by Cissy's biographers and Felicia. Photographs of Cal in Washington, D.C. and the Dower House in Maryland show him formally dressed in suits. In his final years, though, Cal tended to be more unkempt and disheveled in appearance, thus giving Cissy's biographer's and Felicia some credibility on this matter, perhaps. To put the issue in perspective, in *Glass Houses* (p255), Cissy writes about the smells of "leather...and strong, healthy and unwashed men" and is clearly not offended by those odors.

4 Martin, R.G. 1979... op.cit.

5 Ibid.

6 Ibid.

Chapter 15

1 Flat Creek Ranch website (primary source was a National Archive document.) The website is updated occasionally, adding new or different information.

2 Forest Homestead Act 1906 and 1912 Amendment.

3 Flat Creek website (from National Archives).

4 Martin, R.G. "Letters to Rose." *Teton Magazine*. (Vol. 12,1979): 8-11, 27-28, 44-62.

5 National Archives (given in the Flat Creek Ranch history on their website)

6 Ibid.

7 Ibid. Also BLM-GLO website.

8 Teton County, Wyoming, Courthouse Deed and Patent Records bill of sale lists the amount and date. But the story passed on by locals and others was one of great reluctance and hand wringing by Cal, with much pressure being put on him by Cissy to sell, and with Cissy finally sending George Ross to Bates to retrieve the deed from Cal's trunk. See: F. Gizycka. *Forgiveness at Flat Creek*, 1988, where this myth is recorded.

9 Gizycka, F. "Forgiveness at Flat Creek." *Teton Magazine*. (Vol. 20, 1988): 27.

10 Gillette, W. *The Memorable Character...* 1979, op.cit.

11 Gillette, B. *Homesteading with the Elk*. Jackson Printing, 1992.

12 Gizycka, F. *Forgiveness...* 1988, op.cit.

13 Furniss, O. Pers. comm. w/author, 2004.

Chapter 16

1 Burt, S. "The Most Unforgettable Character I've Met." *Reader's Digest.* (Oct 1948): 83-86.

2 Martin, R.G. "Letters to Rose." *Teton Magazine.* (Vol. 12, 1979): 8-11, 27-28, 44-62.

3 Felicia donated them to the Jackson Hole museum, where they are sometimes on display.

4 Gizycka, F. "Diary on the Salmon River." *Teton Magazine.* (Vol. 23 & 24, 1991): 11-12, 34-40. Apparently unknown to Felicia, Cissy also published her river trip diary in *Field and Stream* in May/June 1923. The pen name "Ben" is also used by Cissy for Cal in *Glass Houses*.

5 Ibid.

6 Burt, S. *The Most Unforgettable...* 1948, op.cit.

7 Gizycka, F. *Diary on the Salmon...* 1991, op.cit. This is also mentioned in *Glass Houses* by Cissy.

8 Ibid. Cissy confirms the taking of mountain goats in *Glass Houses*, p70. She also mentions moose and bighorn sheep from Canada and deer and elk from Wyoming, all of which she had trophy heads mounted and hung on her wall in an Eastern residence.

9 Peterson, C. Sr. Pers. comm. w/author, 2004.

10 Bonney and Bonney, 1972, op.cit.

11 Interview with C. Peterson in which he showed the author the articles by O'Conner in *Outdoor Life* magazines.

12 Martin, R.G. *Cissy...* 1979, op.cit.; and, Burt, S. *The Most*

Unforgettable... 1948, op.cit. re. ...loosening up on reins.

13 Hoge, A.A. *Cissy Patterson: The Life of Eleanor Medill Patterson, Publisher and Editor of the Washington Times-Herald.* Random House (1966): 63

14 Martin, R.G. *Cissy...* 1979, op.cit. Also in *Glass Houses*, pp190-195.

15 Martin, R.G. *Letters to Rose...* 1979, op.cit.

16 Martin, R.G. *Cissy...* 1979, op.cit.

Chapter 17

1 Gizycka, F. "Jackson Hole, 1916-65: A Reminiscence." *Vogue.* (April 1, 1965): 203.

2 Martin, R.G. *Cissy: The Extraordinary Life of Eleanor Medill Patterson.* Simon and Shuster, 1979.

3 University of Wyoming interview, 1957.

4 Martin, R.G. 1979, op.cit.

5 Gizycka, F. "Forgiveness at Flat Creek." *Teton Magazine.* (Vol.20, 1988): 29.

6 Gizycka, F. *Jackson Hole, 1916-65...* 1965; and Gizycka, F. "Cissy Patterson: The Countess of Flat Creek." *Teton Magazine.* (Vol.10, 1977): 43.

7 Ibid. 206.

8 Gizycka, F. "Cissy Patterson: The Countess of Flat Creek." *Teton Magazine.* (Vol.10, 1977): 37-48; and Gizycka, F. "Forgiveness at Flat Creek." *Teton Magazine.* (Vol.20, 1988): 29.

9 Rudd, R. Pers. comm. w/author, 2004. Rudd was a

264 I Always Did Like Horses & Women

personal acquaintance of Felicia.

10 Daugherty, J. *A Place Called Jackson Hole*. National Park Service Moose, 1999.

11 In 2005 Chief of Assessor Records, Brian Salmon, searched the San Diego County records from 1914-30 and found no record of Cal's ownership or purchase of the Encinitas property. There was a fire that destroyed some records from that time period, too. However, a 1961 distribution order of the real property inherited by Mary Ake was found, describing the properties. Either Cal purchased the properties after 1930 or he never recorded the purchase or deed. Knowing how Cal did business, it's likely the property transfers were never recorded. Goldie Chisman may also have played a role in assisting Cal in the purchase of his California properties (see letters in the Felicia Gizycka Collection).

12 Martin, R.G. *Cissy*...(1979): 215.

13 Gizycka, F. *Jackson Hole, 1916-65*... (1965): 206. See: Dannatt, A. "Obituary: Countess Felicia Gizycka." *The Independent*, London, 1999, for more detail on Felicia's life.

14 Stone, D. Recorded oral interview, 1958.

15 *Jackson Hole Guide*, Cal Carrington Obituary, December 24, 1959. Jay Lawson, *Men to Match our Mountains*, p53, points out that it took something exceptional to stand out as a hunter in the early twentieth century, since nearly everyone in rural Wyoming hunted for a portion of their subsistence.

16 Stone, D. Recorded oral interview, 1958.

Chapter 18

1 Martin, R.G. "Letters to Rose." *Teton Magazine*. (Vol. 12, 1979): 8-11, 27-28, 44-62. There is some belief, too, that Elmer Schlesinger was happy to have Cal gone because he was generally obnoxiously rude to Elmer.

2 Ibid.

3 Burt, S. "The Most Unforgettable Character I've Met." *Reader's Digest*. (Oct 1948): 83-86. In 1957 Cal wrote to Goldie Chisman about his Africa hunting and said the Natives had called him "never-miss." He also described his excitement about hunting in Africa and shooting hippos from boats at close range (letter in the Felicia Gizycka Colletion).

4 Gillette, W. "The Memorable Character-Cal Carrington." *A Quarterly of Idaho History. Snake River Echoes*, Teton Co. Ed. (Vol. 8, No.3, 1979): 54-62. Gillette provides additional narrative regarding Cal's Africa hunt about the natives gorging themselves on elephant meat after a kill, etc. (taken from the 1958 Stone interview), which has not been included here.

5 Stone, D. Oral interview, 1958.

6 A letter by Cal from Jackson (in the Felicia Gizycka Collection) to Goldie is dated January 7, 1928; in it he writes about earlier retrieving his African trophies at the Victor train station. Previously published accounts say Cal was in Africa for two years, but it could have actually only been a year at most based on his letters dated in the U.S., and depending on when he actually departed in 1927.

7 Gressley, G. Pers. Comm. w/author, 2007. Also others interviewed in Teton valley who told of listening to Cal's African tales and January 7, 1928, letter to Goldie Chisman in Felicia Gizycka Collection.

8 U.S. Census 1930. Ancestry.com.

Chapter 19

1 Burt, S. *The Diary of a Dude Wrangler.* Charles Scribner's Sons. (1924): 306-07.

2 Ibid.

3 Ibid.

4 Ibid.

5 Ibid.

6 Ibid.

7 Gizycka, F. "Cissy Patterson: The Countess of Flat Creek." *Teton Magazine.* (Vol. 10, 1977): 44.

8 Gizycka, E. *Glass Houses* (1926): 146.

Chapter 20

1 Daugherty, J. *A Place Called Jackson Hole.* National Park Service. Moose, 1999.

2 Peterson, C. Sr. Transcribed interview on file at Jackson Hole Historical Society.

3 Wilkinson, T. "Gov Made Poor Pick for G&F Commission." *Jackson Hole News and Guide*, (March 9, 2005): 6A

4 Chambers, R. Pers. comm. w/author, 2004.

5 Ryan, J. Pers. comm. w/author, 2004.

6 Furniss, O. Pers. comm. w/author, 2004.

7 April 25, 1931 letter to Goldie, Felicia Gizycka Collection.

8 Hansen, C. Pers. comm. w/author, 2004.

9 Rudd, R. Pers. comm. w/author, 2004.

10 Martin, R.G. *Cissy: The Extraordinary Life of Eleanor Medill Patterson.* Simon and Schuster, 1979. I have pretty much left Martin's description of Cal's checking on the ranch as he told it. It's a good tale. But in a July 1931 letter to Goldie, Cal himself gives what appears to be his own version about going up to the ranch: "The Countes had a lot of foundations put under her cabans, and I went up thair and got the men all sore at me...but believe they got through quicker. the Watchman [however,] said he was a going quit..." (Felicia Gizycka Collection). The watchman Cal refers to was likely Forney Cole.

11 Furniss, O. Pers. comm.w/author, 2004. Cal was referred to in this manner by several of the LDS people interviewed in Teton Valley.

12 Thompson, G. Pers. comm. w/author, 2004.

13 Breckenridge, D. Pers. comm. w/author, 2004.

14 Furniss, O. Pers. comm. w/author, 2004.

15 Furniss, O. and F. Buxton. Pers. comm. w/author, 2004. Cal apparently liked to grandstand by killing flies with a swatter made from a rhino or elephant's tail, while telling his stories about Africa.

16 Furniss, O. Pers. comm. w/author, 2004.

17 Ibid.

18 April 27, 1941, Carrington letter to Goldie, Felicia Gizycka Collection.

19 Piquet, M. Pers. comm..w/author, 2008.

20 January 18, 1938, letter to Goldie, Felicia Gizycka Collection.

Chapter 21

1 Furniss, O. Pers. comm. w/author, 2004.

2 Ibid.

3 W. Gillette, *The Memorable Character...* 1979, and S. Burt, *The Most Unforgettable Character...* 1948 record the incident in detail. Gillette interviewed Teton Valley residents who were involved. Burt's version was told to him by Cal. The story of the accident is condensed here, but it is an event in Cal's life that was recorded in detail.

4 Burt, S. *The Most Unforgettable Character...* (1948): 84, op.cit.

5 On file at Teton Idaho County Courthouse, Deed and Patent Records. Cal recorded a warranty deed for his Bates property sale for one-dollar to Eleanor Patterson on October 31, 1941, at the Teton County, Idaho, courthouse in Driggs.

Chapter 22

1 Betts, R.B. *Along the Ramparts of the Tetons.* Colorado Assoc. Univ. Press, Boulder, CO, 1978.

2 Martin, R. G. "Letters to Rose." *Teton Magazine.* (Vol. 12, 1979): 8-11, 27-28, 544-62. Martin does not say which President Rose met, but it was most likely Taft, since he

was a friend of the Patterson family.

3 Ibid. According to biographer Amanda Smith, the circumstances of Cissy's death may not have been as straightforward as earlier biographers have described. Martin's story of Cissy's illness and her asking to have her pullman prepared to take her to Jackson one last time may be just that—a good story. No doubt, in fact, she did wish or long to return to those earlier times.

4 May 1948 letter to Goldie, Felicia Gizycka Collection.

5 Gizycka, F. *Jackson Hole, 1916-65,* 1965; *A Reminiscence...,* 208.

6 Teton County, Idaho, courthouse, Deed and Patent Records, op.cit.

7 Gizycka, F. 1977. Cissy Patterson: The Countess of Flat Creek. *Teton Magazine.* Vol. 10, p45. Cal apparently showed Felicia one of Cissy's letters at one point in which the phrase "his cabin" was used. The letter, however, does not appear to be in the Felicia Gizycka Collection currently housed in San Diego.

8 Teton County, Wyoming, Deed and Patent Records.

9 Gizycka, F. *Jackson Hole, 1916-65...* (1965): 206. Felicia's story about Cal's contentious claim for six acres and the cabin may reflect her own mood and earlier legal involvement. She fails to mention her acrimonious contesting of Cissy's will and the fact that the reason Cal was back East several times around that time was because he was summoned for deposition or hearings. In a September 16, 1951, letter to Goldie, Cal writes, "...they are having more trouble over Mrs.

Patterson's estate. So I came to show up again [in Washington, D.C.], it is not very pleasant." (Felicia Gizycka Collection). In short, if Cal did strongly express that six acres and the cabin were his to Felicia, it may well have been within the context of her ongoing contesting of Cissy's will, too. And his travel East, "to ask Felicia for assistance in the matter," as she describes, in reality, may have not been solely for that reason, but rather because he was summoned to appear on her behalf.

10 Gizycka, F. "Cissy Patterson; The Countess of Flat Creek." *Teton Magazine*. (Vol. 10, 1977): 45.

11 Cal Carrington, 5 Aug 1952, letter to Josephine Albright.

12 A June 17, 1959, letter by Cal to Felicia states, "I was up to the cabin on Flat Creek about a month ago and locked it up..." (Felicia Gizycka Collection). The circumstances that had Cal believe he had a claim to the cabin and six acres may have in actuality been more substantial than what we have earlier been led to believe, but it's difficult to prove at this point.

13 Buxton, F. Pers. comm w/author, 2004.

14 Furniss, E. Pers. comm. w/author, 2007.

15 Unpublished draft of *Tales of the Big Hole Mountains* compiled by H. Forbush.

16 Forbush, H. Pers. Comm. w/author, 2004.

17 Gizycka, F. *Jackson Hole, 1916-65...* (1965): 206.

18 Stone, R. Pers. comm. w/author, 2004.

19 Gizycka, F. *Jackson Hole, 1916-65...* (1965): 206.

Chapter 23

1 Gizycka, F. "John Wort and Cal Carrington." *Teton Magazine.* (Vol. 14, 1981): 11.

2 Furniss, O. Pers. comm. w/author, 2004.

3 Breckenridge, D. Pers. comm. w/author, 2004. Cal's Encinitas property holdings were verified through San Diego probate records on file at the country assessor's office. But the date of purchase, when Cal obtained the properties, could not be determined. When he actually began spending winters there isn't known for certain. It's thought beginning around the 1950s. However, his correspondence with Goldie (Felicia Gizycka Collection) indicates a long association with the San Diego area. There is some indication Goldie worked in real estate. Cal had other friends there too, which he refers to: Leanharts and a Mrs. Hillman. In the winter of 1941, he wrote Goldie, "I don't think I will come to San Diego this winter." Instead he spent time in Mountain Home, Idaho. Mountain Home has a relatively mild winter climate and was also a place he used to escape the hard winters of Teton Valley or Jackson.

4 Piquet, M. Pers. comm. w/author, 2008.

5 September 28, 1952, letter to Goldie, Felicia Gizycka Collection.

6 Buxton, F. Pers. comm. w/author, 2004.

Chapter 24

1 Forbush, H. Pers. Comm. w/author, 2004. Forbush believed that Cal lived without any modern conveniences,

perhaps to save money. Felicia called his cabin a "hovel." But Oren Furniss thought Cal did have electricity and a spring for water. The fact Cal bought a radio in 1941 indicates he did have electricity at that time.

2 Breckenridge, D. Pers. comm. w/author, 2004.

3 Gizycka, F. *Jackson Hole, 1916-65...* (1965): 206.

4 Ibid.

5 Gizycka, F. *Cissy Patterson, The Countess...* (1977): 45.

6 Ibid.

7 Ibid, 46. But Cal did continue to go back and use the cabin as evidenced by correspondence to Goldie and Felicia in the Felicia Gizycka Collection. Cal was also probably keyed up and angry at just the confrontation with Remington, too.

8 Ibid.

9 Albright, J. Pers. comm. w/author, 2004.

10 Gizycka, F. (1977): 46.

11 Ibid.

Chapter 25

1 Buxton, F. Pers. comm w/author, 2004.

2 Ibid.

3 Kreps, B. Windows to the Past: Early Settlers in Jackson Hole. JHHM, Jackson (2006): 68.

4 August 5, 1952, letter from Carrington to Josephine Albright.

5 Gizycka, F. "John Wort and Cal Carrington." *Teton*

Magazine. (Vol. 14, 1981): p10-11, 56.

6 Shultz, M. Pers. Comm. w/author, 2007.

7 Gizycka, F. *Jackson Hole, 1916-65...* (1965): 209.

8 Felicia Gizycka Collection, op.cit.

9 Gillette, W. *The Memorable Character...*op.cit.

10 Gizycka, F. op.cit.

11 Ibid, 210, "...my grass is green and tall" statement meant Cal felt he had done well financially (and in life) and he distrusted the reason his siblings were showing up, believing that it was to try to win him over in his last years to share his financial wealth with them. There is evidence Zeneiph Julin tried to make contact with Cal as early as 1946 (see February 19, 1960 Earle and Sadie Harris letter in the Felicia Gizycka Collection).

12 Ibid.

13 E.C. Carrington 17 Dec 1959. Last Will and Testament. State of Wyoming, Cheyenne, Archives.

14 Teton County, Idaho, courthouse records.

15 Bressley, G. Pers. Comm. w/ author, 2007.

16 Gizycka, F. *Jackson Hole, 1916-65...* (1965): 209. In a 12/10/1959 letter to Felicia, Earl Harris describes in detail Cal's battle to reclaim his health, including going to St. Anthony for electrical shock treatments and sweat baths, while giving up his prescribed medications and special diet. Earl Harris said Cal "looked like hell" when he returned from those treatments. He checked into the Driggs hospital again some days afterwards. Harris wrote, "Cal is still anxious to be independent, so makes it a little

difficult." Felicia Gizycka Collection, Cal's November 12, 1959 letter to Goldie and Earl Harris December 10, 1959 letter to Felicia. Those letters are also the primary source material on Cal's childhood.

17 Ibid.

18 Ibid.

19 Ibid. Cal had been closed mouth about his childhood and birth place even with Felicia up until near the very end. It had always been a taboo subject for him with anyone. He finally opened up to Earl Harris, who documented what Cal told him in letters to Felicia and also in conversation to her (Felicia Gizycka Collection). See also: University of Wyoming 1957 interview transcription where Cal says, "That subject is out..." The impression Cal was hiding something was right. But it wasn't necessarily an outlaw past, it was about his family. He refused to talk about them until the very end of his life.

20 Gizycka, F. "John Wort and Cal Carrington." *Teton Magazine.* (Vol. 14, 1981): 56.

21 Ibid.

Chapter 26

1 Gizycka, F. "Jackson Hole, 1916-65: A Reminiscence." *Vogue.* (April 1, 1965): 210. It appears Felicia may have removed more from the cabin than just the items she mentions in this article, as evidenced by some of Cal's personal letters showing up fifty years later in the Felicia Gizycka Collection.

2 Teton County, Idaho, Courthouse Probate Records.

3 San Diego Courthouse Probate Records and also Gizycka, F. *Jackson Hole, 1916-65...* 1965, op.cit.

4 Gizycka, F. *Jackson Hole, 1916-65*; and Mary Ake's obituary. The author contacted Montgomery families in the Seattle area in an attempt to locate any Mary Ake relatives. They would be under her sister's married name Montgomery, but had no success in finding any living relatives of Mary's brother-in-law Paul Montgomery.

5 January 1941 letter to Goldie, Felicia Gizycka Collection.

6 Probate records and 1959 Last Will and Testament.

7 Probate records and Pers. comm. w/ Harold Forbush by author, 2004. Also in the Felicia Gizycka Collection.

8 Robert Rudd in 2005 personal communication informed the author that Gillette told him about visiting the cabin and the trunk and its contents being in the attic right after Cal passed away. Felicia wrote, she went to the cabin to retrieve $50 from Cal's boot as he directed her to do. Recently, some of Cal's personal letters have shown up in the Felicia Gizycka Collection. The Collection is currently in the possession of Felicia's granddaughter, Felicia Cameron, in San Diego. It may someday be transferred to the American Heritage Museum at Laramie. The author has not had opportunity to view the entire collection.

9 Gillette, W. "The Memorable Character-Cal Carrington." *A Quarterly of Idaho History. Snake River Echoes*, Teton Co. Ed. (Vol.8, No. 3, 1979): 54-62. Gillette may have left copies of his photographs with the JHHSM. If he did, they had not been accessioned or made available as of this writing. They are printed in his publication, however.

10 Furniss, O. Pers. Comm. w/author, 2004. Oren remarked to the author that "lots of people had thought they might find money hidden there."

Chapter 27

1 Martin, R.G. *Cissy: The Extraordinary Life of Eleanor Medill Patterson.* Simon and Schuster, 1979. This was most likely a reference to Mary Ake, assuming Martin had reviewed Patterson family papers and saw a letter written by Cissy that derides Cal for having had a baby with Mary Ake.

2 Amanda, S. pers. comm. 2008, re: a letter by Cissy in the J.M. Patterson Papers at Lake Forest, IL.

3 Penciled notes by Wendell Gillette and Felicia Magruder (Gizycka), Wort Hotel, 23 Oct 1987. JHHSM Carrington files.

4 Gizycka, F. "Jackson Hole, 1916-65: A Reminiscence." *Vogue.* (April 1, 1965): 200, 203, 205, 208-210.

5 Downer, G. Pers. comm. w/author, 2004.

6 Gillette, B. *Homesteading with the Elk.* Jackson Printing, 1992.

7 Albright, J. Pers. comm. w/author, 2004.

Chapter 28

1 Gizycka, F. "Jackson Hole, 1916-65: A Reminiscence." *Vogue.* (April 1, 1965): 210.

2 Eleanor Patterson's June 3, 1944, letter to Joseph Patterson, Patterson Papers, Lake Forest College, IL.

Bibliography

Sources

Books

Adare, S. *Jackson Hole Uncovered.* Seaside Press (1997): 108-09.

Alexander, T.G. *The Rise of Multiple-Use Management in the Intermountain West: A History of Region 4 of the Forest Service.* USDA Forest Service (FS 399, 1987): 15-53.

Anderson, A.A. *Experiences and Impressions—The Autobiography of Colonel A.A. Anderson.* MacMillan Company, NY (1933): 89-116.

Betts, R.B. *Along The Ramparts of the Tetons.* Colorado Assoc. Univ. Press, Boulder, CO, 1978.

Bonney, O.H. and L.G. Bonney. *Bonney's Guide: Grand Teton National Park and Jackson's Hole.* Houston, TX (Trip 12, 1972): 122-23.

Brown, D. *Wondrous Times on the Frontier.* August House Publ., Little Rock, AR (1991): 86-105.

Burt, N. *Jackson Hole Journal.* Univ. of Oklahoma Press, 1983.

Burt, S. *The Diary of a Dude Wrangler.* Charles Scribner's Sons, 1924.

Calkins, F. *Jackson Hole*. Alfred A. Knopf., NY, 1973.

Daugherty, J. *A Place Called Jackson Hole*. National Park Service, Moose, 1999.

Driggs, B.W. *History of Teton Valley, Idaho*. Arnold Agency, Rexburg, 1970 ed.

Dyke, J.C. *The West of the Texas Kid, 1881-1910; Recollections of Thomas E. Crawford. Norman,* University of Oklahoma Press, 1962.

Forbush, H. *Tales of the Big Hole Mountains*. Idaho Falls, ID, (2000): 115-16.

Gillette, B. *Homesteading With the Elk*. Jackson Printing, Jackson, WY, 1992.

Gizycka, E. *Glass Houses*. Milton, Balch and Company, NY, 1926.

Healy, P.F. *Cissy: A Biography of Elenor M. "Cissy" Patterson*. Doubleday, 1966.

Hoge, A.A. *Cissy: A Biography of Eleanor Medill Patterson Publisher and Editor of the Washington Times-Herald*. Random House, 1966.

Holmes, B.M. *Victor, Idaho, 1889-1989*. Bound mimeo, 1989.

Huyler, J. *And That's the Way it Was in Jackson Hole*. Jackson Hole Hist. Soc. and Museum. Jackson, WY, 2003.

Lawson, J. *Men to Match our Mountains*. Pronghorn Press, Greybull, WY, (2007): 98-100.

Kreps, B. *Windows to the Past: Early Settlers in Jackson Hole*. Jackson Hole Historical Society and Museum, Jackson, WY, (2007): 61-80.

Marsh, S. "Abandoned Trails" in *Stories of the Wild*. (Ed. by Susan Marsh), White Willow Publ., Jackson, WY, (2001): 237-243.

Martin, R.G. *Cissy: The Extraordinary Life of Eleanor Medill Patterson*. Simon and Shuster, NY, 1979.

Moulton, C.V. *Legacy of the Tetons: Homesteading in Jackson Hole*. Tamarack Books, Boise, 1994.

Mumey, N. *The Teton Mountains: Their History and Tradition*. Artcraft Press, Denver, 1947.

Platts, D. *John Cherry: His Lies, Life and Legend*. Bearpaw Press, Jackson, WY, 1991.

_____. *The Cunningham Ranch Incident*. Wilson, WY, 1992.

_____. *Robert Miller: An Enigma*. Wilson, WY, 2003.

_____. *Teton Jackson Chief of Horsethieves*. Pine Hill Press, SD, 2007.

Smith, B, E. Cole, and D. Dobkin. 2004. *Imperfect Pasture*. USF&WS and Grand Teton Nat. His. Assoc., Jackson, WY. 155p.

Thompson, E.M. S. and W. L. Thompson. *Beaver Dick: The Honor and the Heartbreak*. Jelm Mt. Press, Laramie, 1982.

Wilson, C. A. *The Return of the White Indian Boy*. Univ. of Utah Press, Salt Lake City (bound with *The White Indian Boy* by Elijah N. Wilson), (1985): 151-375.

Wister, O. *The Virginian*. MacMillian Co., 1902.

Periodicals

Anderson, M. *Last of Jackson's Hole Horse Thieves. The Westerner.* (August 24, 1929) (The author Mark Anderson was Stanley Baker's cousin). Unpublished copy given to the Bonneys by Rex Ross.

Buchan, D. "Ties to the Past." *Teton Valley Magazine*, Driggs, ID, (Winter 2007-08): 74-83.

Burt, S. "The Most Unforgettable Character I've Met." *Reader's Digest* (Oct 1948): 83-86.

Cheny, L. "The Countess of Flat Creek." *Annals Of WY* (Fall 1983): 28-32.

Draper, R. "21st-Century Cowboys: Why the Spirit Endures." *National Geographic.* December 2007, 114-135.

Gillette, W. "The Memorable Character—Cal Carrington." *A Quarterly of Idaho History. Snake River Echoes*, Teton Co. Ed., Vol. 8:3 (1979): 54-62.

Gizycka, Countess Eleanor. "Diary on the Salmon River." *Teton Magazine*, Vol 23, 11-12, 34-40; Vol. 24. Jackson, WY, 1991.

Gizycka, E. "Diary on the Salmon River." *Field and Stream* (May and June 1923).

_____. (undated copy) "Two Bear." *Field and Stream*, 596-98.

_____. "Sheep Hunting in Alberta." *Field and Stream* (July 1925): 14-15.

Gizycka, F. "Forgiveness at Flat Creek." *Teton Magazine*, vol. 20. (1988): 8-9, 26-32.

_____. "John Wort and Cal Carrington." *Teton Magazine*, vol. 14, (1981): 10-11 & 56.

_____. "Cissy Paterson: The Countess of Flat Creek." *Teton Magazine*, vol. 10. (1977): 37-48.

_____. "Jackson Hole, 1916-65: A Reminiscence." *Vogue* (April 1965): 200, 203, 205, 208-10.

Layser, P. "The Flat Creek Ranch: Old West, New West, But Always the Real West." *Wyoming Homes and Living Magazine*. (Summer 2005): 20-29.

Martin, R.G. "Letters to Rose." *Teton Magazine*, vol. 12. (1979): 8-11, 27-28, 44-62.

Moss, W. "Those Were The Days My Friend." *Teton Valley Top to Bottom*, Driggs, ID. (Winter 2005): 56-61.

_____. "Tracks to the Tetons." *Teton Home and Living*, Driggs, ID. (Fall/Winter 2006): 64-69.

_____. "The Avenues of Driggs Tell a Story." *Teton Valley Top to Bottom*, Driggs, ID. (Summer 2006): 50-55.

_____. "Friend or Faux." *Teton Valley Top to Bottom*, Driggs, ID. (Summer 2003): 62-67.

Odel, R. "Cal and the Countess." *Teton Magazine*. (Summer/Fall 2002): 62-68.

Rees, A. "A Classless Society: Dude Ranching in the Tetons 1908-1955." *Annals of WY*, vol. 77 (2005): 2-21.

Newspapers

Bill Barlows Budget, 8 June, 1892.

Owen, W. "Matterhorn of America: An Attempt to Ascend the Grand Teton Mountain." Reprinted in the *JHHS Chronicle*, vol. XXVI, No. 3, (Fall 2006).

Dannatt, A. "Obituary: Countess Felicia Gizycka." *The Independent*, London, May 18, 1999.

"Obituary, Cal Carrington." *Jackson Hole Courier*. December 31, 1959.

"Obituary, Cal Carrington." *Jackson Hole Guide*. December 24, 1959, Dec 31, 1959.

"Obituary, Cal Carrington." *Teton Valley News*. December 24, 1959, Dec 31, 1959.

Jackson Hole News. Mar 10, 1999.

Owen Collection. "John Carnes Obituary: Pioneer Civil War Vet Passes at 85 Years." (Bonney and Bonney personal files, Kelly, WY.) July 16, 1931.

Wilkerson, T. "Gov Made Poor Pick for G&F Commission." *Jackson Hole News and Guide*. (9 March 2005): 6A.

Interviews and Personal Communication

Albright, J. Pers. Comm. (conversations w/author), Jackson, WY, 2005.

Arnold, D. Pers. Comm. (telephone conversation w/author), Laramie, WY, 2005.

Arnold, J. Pers. Comm. (conversations w/author), Laramie, WY, 2005/2006.

Bonney, L. Pers. Comm. and access to the Bonneys' Carrington notes, Kelly, WY, 2007.

Breckinridge, D. Pers. Comm. (conversation w/author), Tetonia, ID, 2004.

Buxton, F. Pers. Comm. (telephone conversation w/author),

Bates, ID, 2004.

Buxton, J. Pers. Comm. (telephone conversation w/author), St. George, UT, 2004.

Downer, G. Pers. Comm. (telephone conversation w/author), Calif, 2005.

Forbush, H. Pers. Comm. (telephone conversations w/author), Rexburg, ID, 2004.

Furniss, O. Pers. Comm. (conversations w/author), Bates, ID, 2004.

Gillette, B. Pers. Comm. (telephone conversation w/author), Victor, ID, 2004.

Gillette, W. and F. Gizycka. 1987 Interview. Penciled notes re. Cal Carrington on file at Jackson Hole Historical Society, Jackson, WY.

Gressley, Gene M. Pers. Comm. (telephone re. 1957 Carrington University of Wyo. Interview) 2007.

Hansen, C. Recorded oral interview conducted by C. Hansen, G. Bressley, and others at the Univesity of WY, Laramie (transcribed by the Bonneys and filed with their personal notes) 1957. The original tapes may be at the Wyoming Heritage Center, but were not located.

Hansen, C. Pers. Comm. (telephone conversations w/author), Jackson, WY, 2004, 2007 & 2008.

Peterson, C. Interviews in his home by author, Jackson, WY, 2004/2005.

Peterson, C. Transcribed Oral Interviews (Last of the Old West series by Jo Ann Byrd), Jackson Hole Historical Society, Jackson, WY, 1972 & 1982.

Piquet, M. Pers. Comm. (telephone conversation w/author), Idaho Falls, 2008.

Rudd, R. Pers. Comm. (conversations w/author), Wilson, WY, 2005.

Ryan, J. Pers. Comm. (telephone conversation w/author), Jackson, WY, 2005.

Shultz, M. Pers. Comm. (telephone conversation w/author), Jackson, WY, 2007.

Smith, A. Pers. Comm. (telephone conversations and correspondence w/author), Jackson, WY, 2008.

Stone, D. Recorded Interview with Cal Carrington. Tape on file at Teton Valley Historical Society, Driggs, ID, 1958. (Also transcribed in part and on file at Jackson Hole Historical Society.)

Stone, R. Pers. Comm. (telephone conversation w/author), Victor, ID, 2004.

Thompson, G. Pers. Comm. (telephone conversations w/author), Victor, ID, 2004.

Whittlesey, Lee H. Pers. Comm. (telephone conversation re. Yellowstone National Park history) 2007.

Government Publications

Brandegee, T.S. Annual Report *U.S. Geol. Survey*, 1897-98, Re. Teton Forest Reserve. GLO, Wash., DC.

U.S. Fish and Wildlife Service, *National Elk Refuge* (undated). Timeline of the Miller Ranch and National Elk Refuge.

National Archives

USDI BLM General Land Office Records, Desert Entry Case File No. 3116. Wash., DC.

USDI BLM General Land Office Records, Homestead Entry Case File No. 07481. Wash., DC.

US Census Records/Ancestry.com

Online GLO Records (http://www.glorecords.blm.gov/)

State and Local Archives

Jackson Hole Historical Society and Museum, Jackson, WY (Cal Carrington file folder and photographs).

Jackson Hole Historical Society and Museum Files, Maggie McBride, 1896. *My Diary.*

State of Idaho. Hodges, K. Idaho Historical Society Curator and Research Specialist. 2005. (Mary Ake materials and Carrington genealogy research.)

State of Wyoming. Univ. of Wyoming, American Heritage Center. Laramie, WY.

(General – Northern Pacific Railroad, ranching and period photographs. The Carrington tapes were not found, but could still be there somewhere.)

San Diego County, California, Courthouse Records: County Assessor Maps BK 257 and 9764 and Superior Court Petition Settling the Estate of Cal Carrington.

Teton County, Idaho, Courthouse, Deed and Patent Records (the original records were held in St. Anthony, but were transferred to Driggs when Teton County was formed

–includes: naturalization sworn declaration, probate records, decree to quiet Bates title.)

Teton County, Idaho, Courthouse Records of Decreed Water Rights (the original records were held in St. Anthony, but were later transferred to Driggs, Idaho – Mahogany Creek water right).

Teton County, Idaho, Driggs Museum files. Tales of the Big Hole Mountains: Enoch Cal Carrington, (unpublished notes and interviews).

Teton County, Wyoming, Courthouse, Deed and Patent Records (deed recordings and ownership transfers for the Flat Creek Ranch).

Wyoming State Archives, Cheyenne. Last Will and Testament of E.C. Carrington. Teton County District Court Probate File 546.

World Wide Web

http://www.flatcreekranch.com/history.html

http://www.culturaltourism.org/dch.

http://www.Ancestry.com

http://www.wyomingtalesandtrails.com/tetons.html

http://www.cr.nps.gov/history/onlinebooks/grte/chaps.htm

http://ultimatewyoming.com/sectionpages/sec1/Jackson/jackson/html

http://www.idahohistory.net/Ref%20Series/0451.pdf

http://www.glorecords.blm.gov/

http://www.blm.gov/nhp/landfacts/DesertLand.html

http://www.reference.com/browse/wiki/Desert-Land

http://rondiener.com/JHIW.htm (Diener, R.E. *The Jackson Hole Indian War of 1895.* 2006)

http://www.media.utah.edu/UHE/c/Carrington (Summary of Albert Carrington's life and career)

Other

Excerpts from the Hank Crabtree Interview in the Ralph Martin Collection, Boston University, Howard Gotlieb Archival Center (Box 213, F4), by biographer Amanda Smith.

Selected letters from Felicia Gizycka Collection courtesy of the Arnold family through Amanda Smith (at this writing the collection was located with Felicia Cameron in San Diego, California).

Selected letters from the Joseph Medill Patterson Papers, Lake Forest College, Lake Forest, IL, through biographer Amanda Smith.

The Jackson Hole Flat Creek Ranch (Albright family) and the Arnold family in Laramie (Felicia Gizycka's grandchildren) contributed documents, photographs, and personal knowledge.

Carrington Items

Catalogued at the
Jackson Hole Historical Society and Museum
(as of 2007)

Spanish ring bit

Lariat

Quirt

Pipe

Horsehair strap

Branding iron

Coffee grinder

Certificate of Assistant Forest Ranger appointment

Cissy Patterson's angora chaps given to her by Cal Carrington

Brass plaque that was attached to Carrington's original grave marker

About the Author

Earle F. Layser grew up in a rural and mountainous region of Lycoming County, Pennsylvania, at Cedar Run. After completing an enlistment in the military, at age twenty-one, he drove his 1957 Chevrolet to Missoula, Montana, beginning a life-long adventure with the West. He matriculated in forestry at the University of Montana and was a smokejumper. After completing a Master of Science degree at Syracuse, New York, he worked for Federal land and resource management agencies and as a private consultant throughout the western U.S. and Alaska. He has authored a number of scientific research papers on land-use planning, plant ecology and wildlife, including grizzly bear, mountain caribou and a book on the flora of the Pacific Northwest. In 1976, his career brought him to Jackson Hole and the Greater Yellowstone where he discovered a connection that has lasted a lifetime. In 1990, he retired from government service and returned to the Tetons as a natural resources consultant, photographer and writer. He has authored numerous popular articles on Western history, natural history and travel. He and his wife Pattie live with their dog Benji in Alta, Wyoming, on the west slope of the Tetons.

8728477R0

Made in the USA
Charleston, SC
08 July 2011